The Acts of the Apostles

_____

Presented to

_____

Presented by

_____

Date

_____

Occasion

The *Acts* of the *Apostles*

 The Illustrated
International Children's Bible®

Design and Illustration from
Neely Publishing LLC.

Individual contributors:
Keith R. Neely, David Miles, Roberta Neely,
Bridget Harlow and Thomas R. Zuber

A Division of Thomas Nelson Publishers
Since 1798

www.TommyNelson.com
a division of
Thomas Nelson, Inc.
www.thomasnelson.com

Introduction

Welcome! You've just picked up one of the most amazing books of all time, the Holy Bible. This book of the Bible, Matthew, is presented in a way that has never been done before. Want to know how and why we've done it this way? Keep reading to find out!

Our Purpose

We did not want to create just another children's Bible story-book. In other words, we didn't want to have Bible pictures alongside words that are a retelling of God's Word, the Holy Scriptures. We wanted to draw attention to, magnify, and clarify the actual Word of God. In those words lies the power to change the lives of children and adults alike!

"God's word is alive and working." Hebrews 4:12

"But the word of the Lord will live forever." 1 Peter 1:25

In the same way that written illustrations or "word pictures" are used to help make an idea easy to understand and memorable, our visual illustrations will make the actual Word of God easier to understand than ever before.

The Illustrated International Children's Bible®

The International Children's Bible® was the first translation created especially for children. It has been illustrated in a frame-by-frame format style. These realistic images help illustrate the actual Scriptures . . . the events of the Bible. The format helps to carry the reader easily through each story like a visual movie. This not only makes the verses easier to understand, but also easier to memorize!

Actual Scriptures: Yes, that's right . . . the pages of this book are actual Bible verses. On some pages you'll see the characters speaking by the use of a dialog box. The action and setting of the scene is readily apparent by the backgrounds. What a great way to read and learn your Bible! Some of the verses are not a person speaking, so they will be in plain boxes. You might see some small "d's" in the text. These indicate a word that will have a definition in the dictionary found at the back of full ICB Bibles.

Old Testament quotations are shown in a separate treatment. They are in a parchment like background to represent that they are older words, almost like a treasured antique. They will usually have the book, chapter, and verse with them so you can know where they came from in the Old Testament.

> 5 "Tell the people of Jerusalem, 'Your king is coming to you. He is gentle and riding on a donkey. He is on the colt of a donkey.'"
> Isaiah 62:11; Zechariah 9:9

Footnotes appear at the bottom of some pages. They are represented in the Bible verses by a small "n." That will let you know that there is a note at the bottom of the page that gives you a little more information about that word or phrase. Just more information that's helpful to know!

In some chapters and verses there will not be a lot of interaction between Bible characters, but you will see background scenery, maps, and other interesting treatments to help make your Bible reading more fun and helpful. Most Bible storybooks are just that . . . stories retold to make them easier to understand. Never before has actual Bible Scripture been illustrated in this form so that children and adults can immediately read and know what is going on in a certain verse–who was talking, what time of day it was, was it inside or out, who was there. We hope you enjoy reading this Bible and have fun learning along the way!

The Publishers

Look for these other titles coming soon.

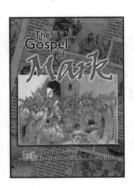

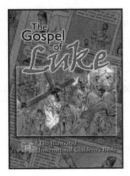

Table of Contents

The Acts of the Apostles

Luke Writes Another Book

1 To Theophilus,
The first book I wrote was about everything that Jesus did and taught. 2 I wrote about the whole life of Jesus, from the beginning until the day he was taken up into heaven. Before this, Jesus talked to the apostles[d] he had chosen. With the help of the Holy Spirit,[d] Jesus told them what they should do. 3 After his death, he showed himself to them and proved in many ways that he was alive.

The apostles saw Jesus during the 40 days after he was raised from death. He spoke to them about the kingdom of God.

4 Once when he was eating with them, he told them not to leave Jerusalem. He said,

"The Father has made you a promise which I told you about before. Wait here to receive this promise. 5 John baptized people with water, but in a few days you will be baptized with the Holy Spirit."

Jesus Is Taken Up into Heaven

6 The apostles[d] were all together. They asked Jesus,

"Lord, are you at this time going to give the kingdom back to Israel?"

7 Jesus said to them,

"The Father is the only One who has the authority to decide dates and times. These things are not for you to know.

8 But the Holy Spirit[d] will come to you. Then you will receive power. You will be my witnesses—in Jerusalem, in all of Judea, in Samaria, and in every part of the world."

9 After he said this, as they were watching, he was lifted up. A cloud hid him from their sight. 10 As he was going, they were looking into the sky. Suddenly, two men wearing white clothes stood beside them.

Acts 1:11-19

11 They said, "Men of Galilee, why are you standing here looking into the sky? You saw Jesus taken away from you into heaven. He will come back in the same way you saw him go."

A New Apostle Is Chosen

12 Then they went back to Jerusalem from the Mount of Olives.[d] (This mountain is about half a mile from Jerusalem.) 13 When they entered the city, they went to the upstairs room where they were staying.

Peter, John, James, Andrew, Philip, Thomas, Bartholomew, Matthew, James son of Alphaeus, Simon (known as the Zealot[d]), and Judas son of James were there.

14 They all continued praying together. Some women, including Mary the mother of Jesus, and Jesus' brothers were also there with the apostles.

15 During this time there was a meeting of the believers. (There were about 120 of them.) Peter stood up and said,

16-17 "Brothers, in the Scriptures[d] the Holy Spirit[d] said through David that something must happen. The Spirit was talking about Judas, one of our own group, who served together with us. The Spirit said that Judas would lead men to arrest Jesus.

18 (Judas bought a field with the money he got for his evil act. But Judas fell to his death, his body burst open, and all his intestines poured out.

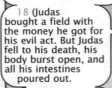

19 Everyone in Jerusalem learned about this. This is why they named the field Akeldama. In their language Akeldama means "field of blood.")

20 "In the book of Psalms, this is written:

'May his place be empty. Leave no one to live in it.'

Psalm 69:25

And it is also written:

'Let another man replace him as leader.'

Psalm 109:8

21-22 "So now a man must join us and become a witness of Jesus' being raised from death. He must be one of the men who were part of our group during all the time the Lord Jesus was with us. He must have been with us from the time John began to baptize people until the day when Jesus was taken up from us to heaven."

23 They put the names of two men before the group. One was Joseph Barsabbas, who was also called Justus.

The other was Matthias.

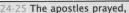
24-25 The apostles prayed,

"Lord, you know the minds of everyone. Show us which one of these two you have chosen to do this work. Judas turned away from it and went where he belongs. Lord, show us which one should take his place as an apostle!"[d]

26 Then they used lots[d] to choose between them,

and the lots showed that Matthias was the one. So he became an apostle with the other 11.

Chapter 2

The Coming of the Holy Spirit

3

Acts 2:1-15

1 When the day of Pentecost[d] came, they were all together in one place. 2 Suddenly a noise came from heaven. It sounded like a strong wind blowing. This noise filled the whole house where they were sitting. 3 They saw something that looked like flames of fire.

The flames were separated and stood over each person there.

4 They were all filled with the Holy Spirit[d] and they began to speak different languages. The Holy Spirit was giving them the power to speak these languages.

5 There were some religious Jews staying in Jerusalem who were from every country in the world. 6 When they heard this noise, a crowd came together. They were all surprised, because each one heard them speaking in his own language. 7 They were completely amazed at this. They said,

"Look! Aren't all these men that we hear speaking from Galilee?[n]"

8 But each of us hears them in his own language. How is this possible? We are from different places:

9 Parthia, Media, Elam, Mesopotamia, Judea, Cappadocia, Pontus, Asia, 10 Phrygia, Pamphylia, Egypt, the areas of Libya near Cyrene, Rome 11 (both Jews and those who had become Jews), Crete and Arabia. But we hear these men telling in our own languages about the great things God has done!"

12 They were all amazed and confused. They asked each other,

"What does this mean?"

13 But others were making fun of them, saying,

"They have had too much wine."

Peter Speaks to the People

14 But Peter stood up with the 11 apostles.[d] In a loud voice he spoke to the crowd:

"My fellow Jews, and all of you who are in Jerusalem, listen to me. Pay attention to what I have to say. 15 These men are not drunk, as you think; it is only nine o'clock in the morning!

2:7 from Galilee The people thought men from Galilee could speak only their own language.

16 "But Joel the prophet[d] wrote about what is happening here today:

17 'God says: In the last days I will give my Spirit[d] freely to all kinds of people. Your sons and daughters will prophesy.[d] Your old men will dream dreams. Your young men will see visions. 18 At that time I will give my Spirit even to my servants, both men and women. And they will prophesy. 19 I will show miracles[d] in the sky and on the earth: blood, fire and thick smoke. 20 The sun will become dark. The moon will become red as blood. And then the great and glorious day of the Lord will come. 21 Then anyone who asks the Lord for help will be saved.'

Joel 2:28-32

22 "Men of Israel, listen to these words: Jesus from Nazareth was a very special man. God clearly showed this to you by the miracles,[d] wonders, and signs God did through him. You all know this, because it happened right here among you. 23 Jesus was given to you, and you killed him. With the help of evil men you nailed him to a cross.

But God knew all this would happen. This was God's plan which he had made long ago. 24 God raised Jesus from death. God set him free from the pain of death. Death could not hold him. 25 For David said this about him:

'I keep the Lord before me always. Because he is close by my side, I will not be hurt. 26 So I am glad, and I rejoice. Even my body has hope. 27 This is because you will not leave me in the grave. You will not let your Holy One rot. 28 You will teach me God's way to live. Being with you will fill me with joy.' Psalm 16:8-11

29 "Brothers, I can tell you truly about David, our ancestor. He died and was buried. His grave is still here with us today. 30 David was a prophet[d] and knew what God had said. God had promised David that he would make a person from David's family a king just as he was.[n] 31 David knew this before it happened. That is why he said:

'He was not left in the grave. His body did not rot.'

David was talking about the Christ[d] rising from death.

32 So Jesus is the One who God raised from death! And we are all witnesses to this. 33 Jesus was lifted up to heaven and is now at God's right side. The Father has given the Holy Spirit[d] to Jesus as he promised. So now Jesus has poured out that Spirit. This is what you see and hear. 34 David was not the one who was lifted up to heaven.

But he said:

'The Lord said to my Lord: Sit by me at my right side, 35 until I put your enemies under your control.'[n] Psalm 110:1

36 "So, all the people of Israel should know this truly: God has made Jesus both Lord and Christ. He is the man you nailed to the cross!"

2:30 God . . . was. See 2 Samuel 7:13; Psalm 132:11.
2:35 until . . . control Literally, "until I make your enemies a footstool for your feet."

5

Acts 2:37-47

37 When the people heard this, they were sick at heart.

They asked Peter and the other apostles,

"What shall we do?"

38 Peter said to them,

"Change your hearts and lives and be baptized, each one of you, in the name of Jesus Christ for the forgiveness of your sins. And you will receive the gift of the Holy Spirit. 39 This promise is for you. It is also for your children and for all who are far away. It is for everyone the Lord our God calls to himself."

40 Peter warned them with many other words. He begged,

"Save yourselves from the evil of today's people!"

41 Then those people who accepted what Peter said were baptized.

About 3,000 people were added to the number of believers that day.

42 They spent their time learning the apostles' teaching. And they continued to share,

to break bread,[n] and to pray together.

The Believers Share

43 The apostles[d] were doing many miracles[d] and signs. And everyone felt great respect for God.

44 All the believers stayed together. They shared everything. 45 They sold their land and the things they owned. Then they divided the money and gave it to those people who needed it. 46 The believers met together in the Temple[d] every day. They all had the same purpose. They broke bread in their homes, happy to share their food with joyful hearts. 47 They praised God, and all the people liked them. More and more people were being saved every day; the Lord was adding those people to the group of believers.

2:42 break bread This may mean a meal as in verse 46, or the Lord's Supper, the special meal Jesus told his followers to eat to remember him (Luke 22:14-20).

Chapter 3

Peter Heals a Cripled Man

1 One day Peter and John went to the Temple.ᵈ It was three o'clock in the afternoon. This was the time for the daily prayer service. 2 There, at the Temple gate called Beautiful Gate, was a man who had been crippled all his life. Every day he was carried to this gate to beg. He would ask for money from the people going into the Temple. 3 The man saw Peter and John going into the Temple and asked them for money. 4 Peter and John looked straight at him and said,

"Look at us!"

5 The man looked at them; he thought they were going to give him some money.

6 But Peter said,

"I don't have any silver or gold, but I do have something else I can give you: By the power of Jesus Christ from Nazareth—stand up and walk!"

7 Then Peter took the man's right hand and lifted him up.

Immediately the man's feet and ankles became strong. 8 He jumped up, stood on his feet, and began to walk.

He went into the Temple with them, walking and jumping, and praising God.

9-10 All the people recognized him. They knew he was the crippled man who always sat by the Beautiful Gate begging for money. Now they saw this same man walking and praising God. The people were amazed. They could not understand how this could happen.

Peter Speaks to the People

11 The man was holding on to Peter and John. All the people were amazed and ran to Peter and John at Solomon's Porch.ᵈ 12 When Peter saw this, he said to them,

"Men of Israel, why are you surprised? You are looking at us as if it were our own power that made this man walk. Do you think this happened because we are good? No! 13 The God of Abraham, Isaac and Jacob, the God of our ancestors, gave glory to Jesus, his servant. But you gave him up to be killed. Pilate decided to let him go free. But you told Pilate you did not want Jesus.

7

Acts 3:14-26

14 "He was pure and good, but you said you did not want him. You told Pilate to give you a murderer[n] instead of Jesus. 15 And so you killed the One who gives life! But God raised him from death. We are witnesses to this. 16 It was the power of Jesus that made this crippled man well. This happened because we trusted in the power of Jesus. You can see this man, and you know him. He was made completely well because of trust in Jesus. You all saw it happen!

17 "Brothers, I know you did those things to Jesus because you did not understand what you were doing. Your leaders did not understand either. 18 God said this would happen. He said through the prophets[d] that his Christ[d] would suffer and die. And now God has made these things come true in this way.

19 So you must change your hearts and lives! Come back to God, and he will forgive your sins.

20 Then the Lord will give you times of spiritual rest. He will give you Jesus, the One he chose to be the Christ.

21 But Jesus must stay in heaven until the time comes when all things will be made right again. God told about this time long ago when he spoke through his holy prophets. 22 Moses said, 'The Lord your God will give you a prophet like me. He will be one of your own people. You must obey everything he tells you. 23 Anyone who does not obey him will die, separated from God's people.'[n] 24 Samuel, and all the other prophets who spoke for God after Samuel, told about this time now.

25 You have received what the prophets talked about. You have received the agreement God made with your ancestors. He said to your father Abraham, 'Through your descendants[d] all the nations on the earth will be blessed.'[n]

26 God has raised up his servant and sent him to you first. He sent Jesus to bless you by turning each of you away from doing evil things."

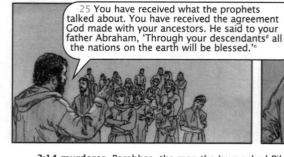
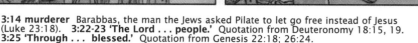

3:14 murderer Barabbas, the man the Jews asked Pilate to let go free instead of Jesus (Luke 23:18). **3:22-23 'The Lord . . . people.'** Quotation from Deuteronomy 18:15, 19. **3:25 'Through . . . blessed.'** Quotation from Genesis 22:18; 26:24.

Chapter 4

Peter and John at the Council

1 While Peter and John were speaking to the people, a group of men came up to them. There were Jewish priests, the captain of the soldiers that guarded the Temple,[d] and some Sadducees.[d] 2 They were upset because the two apostles[d] were teaching the people. Peter and John were preaching that people will rise from death through the power of Jesus.

3 The Jewish leaders grabbed Peter and John and put them in jail. It was already night, so they kept them in jail until the next day. 4 But many of those who heard Peter and John preach believed the things they said. There were now about 5,000 men in the group of believers.

5 The next day the Jewish rulers, the Jewish elders, and the teachers of the law met in Jerusalem.

6 Annas the high priest, Caiaphas, John, and Alexander were there. Everyone from the high priest's family was there.

7 They made Peter and John stand before them. The Jewish leaders asked them:

"By what power or authority did you do this?"

8 Then Peter was filled with the Holy Spirit.[d] He said to them,

"Rulers of the people and you elders,

9 are you questioning us about a good thing that was done to a crippled man? Are you asking us who made him well? 10 We want all of you and all the Jewish people to know that this man was made well by the power of Jesus Christ from Nazareth! You nailed him to a cross, but God raised him from death. This man was crippled, but he is now well and able to stand here before you because of the power of Jesus!

11 Jesus is

'the stone[n] that you builders did not want. It has become the cornerstone.'[d]   *Psalm 118:22*

12 Jesus is the only One who can save people. No one else in the world is able to save us."

13 The Jewish leaders saw that Peter and John were not afraid to speak. They understood that these men had no special training or education. So they were amazed. Then they realized that Peter and John had been with Jesus.

14 They saw the crippled man standing there beside the two apostles. They saw that the man was healed. So they could say nothing against them. 15 The Jewish leaders told them to leave the meeting. Then the leaders talked to each other about what they should do. 16 They said,

"What shall we do with these men?

17 But we must warn them not to talk to people anymore using that name.

Everyone in Jerusalem knows that they have done a great miracle![d] We cannot say it is not true.

4:11 stone A symbol meaning Jesus.

"Then this thing will not spread among the people."

18 So they called Peter and John in again. They told them not to speak or to teach at all in the name of Jesus. 19 But Peter and John answered them,

"What do you think is right? What would God want? Should we obey you or God?

21-22 The Jewish leaders could not find a way to punish them because all the people were praising God for what had been done. (This miracle was a proof from God. The man who was healed was more than 40 years old!) So the Jewish leaders warned the apostles again and let them go free.

20 We cannot keep quiet. We must speak about what we have seen and heard."

The Believers' Prayer

23 Peter and John left the meeting of Jewish leaders and went to their own group. They told them everything that the leading priests and the Jewish elders had said to them. 24 When the believers heard this, they prayed to God with one purpose. They prayed,

"Lord, you are the One who made the sky, the earth, the sea, and everything in the world. 25 Our father David was your servant. With the help of the Holy Spirit[d] he said:

'Why are the nations so angry? Why are the people making useless plans? 26 The kings of the earth prepare to fight. Their leaders make plans together against the Lord and against his Christ.'[d]
Psalm 2:1-2

11

27 "These things really happened when Herod, Pontius Pilate, the non-Jewish people, and the Jewish people all came together against Jesus here in Jerusalem. Jesus is your holy Servant. He is the One you made to be the Christ. 28 These people made your plan happen; it happened because of your power and your will. 29 And now, Lord, listen to what they are saying. They are trying to make us afraid! Lord, we are your servants. Help us to speak your word without fear.

30 Help us to be brave by showing us your power; make sick people well, give proofs, and make miracles[d] happen by the power of Jesus, your holy servant."

31 After they had prayed, the place where they were meeting was shaken. They were all filled with the Holy Spirit,[d] and they spoke God's word without fear.

The Believers Share

32 The group of believers were joined in their hearts, and they had the same spirit. No person in the group said that the things he had were his own. Instead, they shared everything. 33 With great power the apostles[d] were telling people that the Lord Jesus was truly raised from death. And God blessed all the believers very much. 34 They all received the things they needed. Everyone that owned fields or houses sold them. They brought the money

35 and gave it to the apostles. Then each person was given the things he needed. 36 One of the believers was named Joseph. The apostles called him Barnabas. (This name means "one who encourages.") He was a Levite, born in Cyprus. 37 Joseph owned a field. He sold it, brought the money, and gave it to the apostles.

Chapter 5

Ananias and Sapphira

1 A man named Ananias and his wife Sapphira sold some land. 2 But he gave only part of the money to the apostles.[d] He secretly kept some of it for himself. His wife knew about this, and she agreed to it.

3 Peter said,

"Ananias, why did you let Satan rule your heart? You lied to the Holy Spirit.[d] Why did you keep part of the money you received for the land for yourself?

4 Before you sold the land, it belonged to you. And even after you sold it, you could have used the money any way you wanted.

Why did you think of doing this? You lied to God, not to men!"

5-6 When Ananias heard this, he fell down and died.

Some young men came in, wrapped up his body, carried it out, and buried it. And everyone who heard about this was filled with fear.

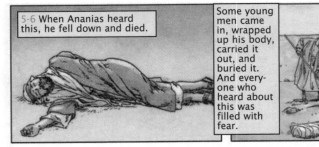

7 About three hours later his wife came in. She did not know what had happened. 8 Peter said to her,

"Tell me how much money you got for your field. Was it this much?"

Sapphira answered,

"Yes, that was the price."

13

Acts 5:9-16

9 Peter said to her,

"Why did you and your husband agree to test the Spirit of the Lord?

Look! The men who buried your husband are at the door! They will carry you out."

10 At that moment Sapphira fell down by his feet and died.

The young men came in and saw that she was dead. They carried her out and buried her beside her husband. 11 The whole church and all the others who heard about these things were filled with fear.

Proofs from God

12 The apostles[d] did many signs and miracles[d] among the people.

And they would all meet together on Solomon's Porch.[d]

13 None of the others dared to stand with them. All the people were saying good things about them.

14 More and more men and women believed in the Lord and were added to the group of believers. 15 As Peter was passing by, the people brought their sick into the streets. They put their sick on beds and mats so at least Peter's shadow might fall on them. 16 Crowds came from all the towns around Jerusalem. They brought their sick and those who were bothered by evil spirits. All of them were healed.

The Apostles Obey God

17 The high priest and all his friends (a group called the Sadducees[d]) became very jealous.

18 They took the apostles[d] and put them in jail.

19 But during the night, an angel of the Lord opened the doors of the jail. He led the apostles outside and said,

20 "Go and stand in the Temple.[d] Tell the people everything about this new life."

21 When the apostles heard this, they obeyed and went into the Temple. It was early in the morning, and they began to teach.

The high priest and his friends arrived. They called a meeting of the Jewish leaders and all the important older men of the Jews. They sent some men to the jail to bring the apostles to them. 22 When the men went to the jail, they could not find the apostles. So they went back and told the Jewish leaders about this. 23 They said,

"The jail was closed and locked. The guards were standing at the doors. But when we opened the doors, the jail was empty!"

24 Hearing this, the captain of the Temple guards and the leading priests were confused. They wondered, "What will happen because of this?" 25 Then someone came and told them,

"Listen! The men you put in jail are standing in the Temple. They are teaching the people!"

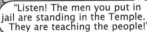

26 Then the captain and his men went out and brought the apostles back. But the soldiers did not use force, because they were afraid that the people would kill them with stones. 27 The soldiers brought the apostles to the meeting and made them stand before the Jewish leaders. The high priest questioned them.

Acts 5:28-36

28 He said,

"We gave you strict orders not to go on teaching in that name. But look what you have done!

You have filled Jerusalem with your teaching. You are trying to make us responsible for this man's death."

29 Peter and the other apostles answered,

"We must obey God, not men! 30 You killed Jesus. You hung him on a cross. But God, the same God our ancestors had, raised Jesus up from death! 31 Jesus is the One whom God raised to be on his right side. God made Jesus our Leader and Savior. God did this so that all Jews could change their hearts and lives and have their sins forgiven. 32 We saw all these things happen. The Holy Spirit[d] also proves that these things are true. God has given the Spirit to all who obey him."

33 When the Jewish leaders heard this, they became very angry and wanted to kill them.

34 A Pharisee[d] named Gamaliel stood up in the meeting. He was a teacher of the law, and all the people respected him. He ordered the apostles to leave the meeting for a little while.

35 Then he said to them,

"Men of Israel, be careful of what you are planning to do to these men! 36 Remember when Theudas appeared? He said that he was a great man, and about 400 men joined him. But he was killed. And all his followers were scattered. They were able to do nothing.

16

37 "Later, a man named Judas came from Galilee at the time of the registration.[n] He led a group of followers, too. He was also killed, and all his followers were scattered. 38 And so now I tell you: Stay away from these men. Leave them alone. If their plan comes from men, it will fail.

39 But if it is from God, you will not be able to stop them. You might even be fighting against God himself!"

The Jewish leaders agreed with what Gamaliel said.

40 They called the apostles in again. They beat the apostles and told them not to speak in the name of Jesus again. Then they let them go free.

41 The apostles left the meeting full of joy because they were given the honor of suffering disgrace for Jesus.

42 The apostles did not stop teaching people. Every day in the Temple and in people's homes they continued to tell the Good News—that Jesus is the Christ.[d]

Chapter

6

Seven Men Are Chosen

1 More and more people were becoming followers of Jesus. But during this same time, the Greek-speaking followers had an argument with the other Jewish followers. The Greek-speaking Jews said that their widows were not getting their share of the food that was given out every day.

5:37 registration Census. A counting of all the people and the things they own.

Acts 6:2-11

2 The 12 apostles[d] called the whole group of followers together. They said, "It is not right for us to stop our work of teaching God's word in order to serve tables. 3 So, brothers, choose seven of your own men. They must be men who are good. They must be full of wisdom and full of the Spirit.[d] We will put them in charge of this work. 4 Then we can use all our time to pray and to teach the word of God."

5 The whole group liked the idea. So they chose these seven men: Stephen (a man with great faith and full of the Holy Spirit), Philip,[n] Procorus, Nicanor, Timon, Parmenas, and Nicolas (a man from Antioch who had become a Jew).

6 Then they put these men before the apostles. The apostles prayed and laid their hands on[n] the men.
7 The word of God was reaching more and more people. The group of followers in Jerusalem became larger and larger. A great number of the Jewish priests believed and obeyed.

Stephen Is Arrested

8 Stephen was richly blessed by God. God gave him the power to do great miracles[d] and signs among the people.

9 But some Jews were against him. They belonged to a synagogue[d] of Free Men[n] (as it was called). (This synagogue was also for Jews from Cyrene and from Alexandria.) Jews from Cilicia and Asia were also with them. They all came and argued with Stephen.
10 But the Spirit[d] was helping him to speak with wisdom. His words were so strong that they could not argue with him. 11 So they paid some men to say,

"We heard him say things against Moses and against God!"

6:5 Philip Not the apostle named Philip. **6:6 laid their hands on** Here, doing this showed that these men were given a special work of God. **6:9 Free Men** Jews who had been slaves or whose fathers had been slaves, but were now free.

12 This upset the people, the Jewish elders, and the teachers of the law. They came to Stephen, grabbed him and brought him to a meeting of the Jewish leaders. 13 They brought in some men to tell lies about Stephen. They said,

"This man is always saying things against this holy place and the law of Moses. 14 We heard him say that Jesus from Nazareth will destroy this place. He also said that Jesus will change the things that Moses told us to do."

15 All the people in the meeting were watching Stephen closely. His face looked like the face of an angel.

Chapter 7

Stephen's Speech

1 The high priest said to Stephen,

"Are these things true?"

2 Stephen answered,

"Brothers and fathers, listen to me.

Our glorious God appeared to Abraham, our ancestor. Abraham was in Mesopotamia before he lived in Haran. 3 God said to Abraham, 'Leave your country and your relatives. Go to the land I will show you.'[n]

7:3 'Leave . . . you.' Quotation from Genesis 12:1.

19

4 "So Abraham left the country of Chaldea and went to live in Haran. After Abraham's father died, God sent him to this place where you now live.

5 God did not give Abraham any of this land, not even a foot of it. But God promised that he would give him and his descendants[d] this land. (This was before Abraham had any descendants.) 6 This is what God said to him: 'Your descendants will be strangers in a land they don't own. The people there will make them slaves. And they will do cruel things to them for 400 years.

7 But I will punish the nation where they are slaves. Then your descendants will leave that land. Then they will worship me in this place.'[n] 8 God made an agreement with Abraham; the sign for this agreement was circumcision.[d] And so when Abraham had his son Isaac, Abraham circumcised him when he was eight days old. Isaac also circumcised his son Jacob.

And Jacob did the same for his sons, the 12 ancestors[n] of our people.
9 "These sons became jealous of Joseph. They sold him to be a slave in Egypt. But God was with him. 10 Joseph had many troubles there, but God saved him from all those troubles. The king of Egypt liked Joseph and respected him because of the wisdom that God gave him. The king made him governor of Egypt. He put Joseph in charge of all the people in his palace.

7:6-7 'Your descendants . . . place.' Quotation from Genesis 15:13-14 and Exodus 3:12.
7:8 12 ancestors Important ancestors of the Jews; the leaders of the 12 Jewish tribes.

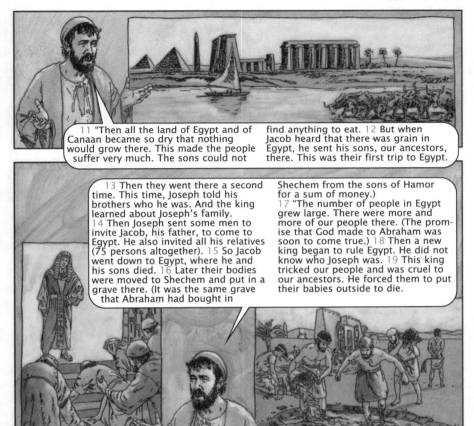

11 "Then all the land of Egypt and of Canaan became so dry that nothing would grow there. This made the people suffer very much. The sons could not find anything to eat. 12 But when Jacob heard that there was grain in Egypt, he sent his sons, our ancestors, there. This was their first trip to Egypt.

13 Then they went there a second time. This time, Joseph told his brothers who he was. And the king learned about Joseph's family. 14 Then Joseph sent some men to invite Jacob, his father, to come to Egypt. He also invited all his relatives (75 persons altogether). 15 So Jacob went down to Egypt, where he and his sons died. 16 Later their bodies were moved to Shechem and put in a grave there. (It was the same grave that Abraham had bought in Shechem from the sons of Hamor for a sum of money.)

17 "The number of people in Egypt grew large. There were more and more of our people there. (The promise that God made to Abraham was soon to come true.) 18 Then a new king began to rule Egypt. He did not know who Joseph was. 19 This king tricked our people and was cruel to our ancestors. He forced them to put their babies outside to die.

20 This was the time when Moses was born. He was a fine child. For three months Moses was cared for in his father's house. 21 When they put Moses outside, the king's daughter took him. She raised him as if he were her own son.

Acts 7:22-32

22 "The Egyptians taught Moses all the things they knew. He was a powerful man in the things he said and did.
23 "When Moses was about 40 years old, he thought it would be good to visit his brothers, the people of Israel. 24 Moses saw an Egyptian doing wrong to a Jew. So he defended the Jew and punished the Egyptian for hurting him. Moses killed the Egyptian.

25 Moses thought that his fellow Jews would understand that God was using him to save them. But they did not understand. 26 The next day, Moses saw two Jewish men fighting. He tried to make peace between them. He said, 'Men, you are brothers! Why are you hurting each other?' 27 The man who was hurting the other man pushed Moses away. He said, 'Who made you our ruler and judge? 28 Are you going to kill me as you killed the Egyptian yesterday?'[n]

29 When Moses heard him say this, he left Egypt. He went to live in the land of Midian where he was a stranger. While Moses lived in Midian, he had two sons. 30 "After 40 years Moses was in the desert near Mount Sinai. An angel appeared to him in the flames of a burning bush.

31 When Moses saw this, he was amazed. He went near to look closer at it. Moses heard the Lord's voice.

32 The Lord said, 'I am the God of your ancestors. I am the God of Abraham, Isaac and Jacob.'[n]

Moses began to shake with fear and was afraid to look.

7:27-28 'Who . . . yesterday?' Quotation from Exodus 2:14.
7:32 'I am . . . Jacob.' Quotation from Exodus 3:6.

33 "The Lord said to him,

'Take off your sandals. You are standing on holy ground. 34 I have seen the troubles my people have suffered in Egypt. I have heard their cries. I have come down to save them. And now, Moses, I am sending you back to Egypt.'ⁿ

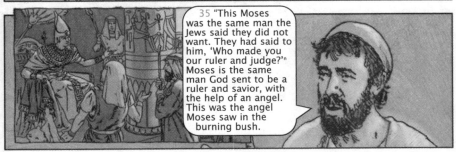

35 "This Moses was the same man the Jews said they did not want. They had said to him, 'Who made you our ruler and judge?'ⁿ Moses is the same man God sent to be a ruler and savior, with the help of an angel. This was the angel Moses saw in the burning bush.

36 So Moses led the people out of Egypt. He worked miraclesᵈ and signs in Egypt, at the Red Sea,ᵈ and then in the desert for 40 years.

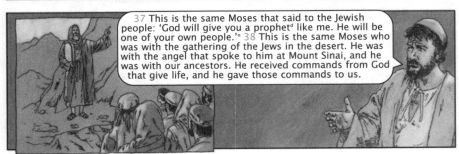

37 This is the same Moses that said to the Jewish people: 'God will give you a prophetᵈ like me. He will be one of your own people.'ⁿ 38 This is the same Moses who was with the gathering of the Jews in the desert. He was with the angel that spoke to him at Mount Sinai, and he was with our ancestors. He received commands from God that give life, and he gave those commands to us.

7:33-34 'Take . . . Egypt.' Quotation from Exodus 3:5-10.
7:35 'Who . . . judge?' Quotation from Exodus 2:14.
7:37 'God . . . people.' Quotation from Deuteronomy 18:15.

39 "But our fathers did not want to obey Moses. They rejected him. They wanted to go back to Egypt again. 40 They said to Aaron, 'Moses led us out of Egypt. But we don't know what has happened to him. So make us gods who will lead us.'ⁿ

41 So the people made an idol that looked like a calf. Then they brought sacrifices to it. The people were proud of what they had made with their own hands!

42 But God turned against them. He did not try to stop them from worshiping the sun, moon and stars. This is what is written in the book of the prophets: God says,

'People of Israel, you did not bring me sacrifices and offerings while you traveled in the desert for 40 years. 43 But now you will have to carry with you the tent to worship the false god Molechᵈ and the idols of the star god Rephan that you made to worship. This is because I will send you away beyond Babylon.'

Amos 5:25-27

44 "The Holy Tentᵈ where God spoke to our fathers was with the Jews in the desert. God told Moses how to make this Tent. He made it like the plan God showed him.

7:40 'Moses . . . us.' Quotation from Exodus 32:1.

24

45 "Later, Joshua led our fathers to capture the lands of the other nations. Our people went in, and God drove the other people out. When our people went into this new land, they took with them this same Tent. They received this Tent from their fathers and kept it until the time of David. 46 God was very pleased with David. He asked God to let him build a house for him, the God of Jacob.ⁿ

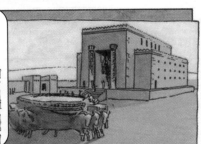

47 But Solomon was the one who built the Temple.ᵈ
48 "But the Most High does not live in houses that men build with their hands. This is what the prophet says:

49 'Heaven is my throne. The earth is my footstool. So do you think you can build a house for me? says the Lord. There is no place where I need to rest. 50 Remember, I made all these things!'" *Isaiah 66:1-2*

51 Stephen continued speaking:

"You stubborn Jewish leaders! You have not given your hearts to God! You won't listen to him! You are always against what the Holy Spiritᵈ is trying to tell you. Your ancestors were like this, and you are just like them! 52 Your fathers tried to hurt every prophet who ever lived. Those prophets said long ago that the Righteous One would come. But your fathers killed them. And now you have turned against the Righteous One and killed him.

53 You received the law of Moses, which God gave you through his angels. But you don't obey it!"

7:46 **the God of Jacob** Some Greek copies read "the house of Jacob." This means the people of Israel.

Stephen Is Killed

54 When the leaders heard Stephen saying all these things, they became very angry. They were so mad that they were grinding their teeth at Stephen. 55 But Stephen was full of the Holy Spirit.[d] He looked up to heaven and saw the glory of God. He saw Jesus standing at God's right side.

56 He said, "Look! I see heaven open. And I see the Son of Man[d] standing at God's right side!"

57 Then they all shouted loudly. They covered their ears with their hands and all ran at Stephen.

58 They took him out of the city and threw stones at him until he was dead.

The men who told lies against Stephen left their coats with a young man named Saul. 59 While they were throwing stones, Stephen prayed,

"Lord Jesus, receive my spirit!"

60 He fell on his knees and cried in a loud voice,

"Lord, do not hold this sin against them!"

After Stephen said this, he died.

Chapter 8

1 Saul agreed that the killing of Stephen was a good thing.

Trouble for the Believers

2-3 Some religious men buried Stephen. They cried very loudly for him. On that day people began trying to hurt the church in Jerusalem and make it suffer.

Saul was also trying to destroy the church. He went from house to house. He dragged out men and women and put them in jail. All the believers, except the apostles,[d] went to different places in Judea and Samaria.

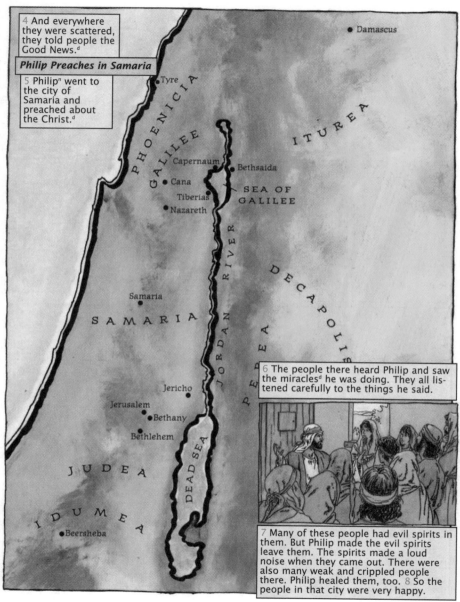

4 And everywhere they were scattered, they told people the Good News.[d]

Philip Preaches in Samaria

5 Philip[n] went to the city of Samaria and preached about the Christ.[d]

6 The people there heard Philip and saw the miracles[d] he was doing. They all listened carefully to the things he said.

7 Many of these people had evil spirits in them. But Philip made the evil spirits leave them. The spirits made a loud noise when they came out. There were also many weak and crippled people there. Philip healed them, too. **8** So the people in that city were very happy.

Damascus

Tyre

PHOENICIA

GALILEE

ITUREA

Capernaum

Bethsaida

Cana

SEA OF GALILEE

Tiberias

Nazareth

DECAPOLIS

JORDAN RIVER

P E R E A

Samaria

SAMARIA

Jericho

Jerusalem

Bethany

Bethlehem

DEAD SEA

J U D E A

I D U M E A

Beersheba

8:5 Philip Not the apostle named Philip.

9 But there was a man named Simon in that city. Before Philip came there, Simon had practiced magic. He amazed all the people of Samaria with his magic. He bragged and called himself a great man. 10 All the people—the least important and the most important—paid attention to what Simon said. They said,

"This man has the power of God, called 'the Great Power'!"

11 Simon had amazed them with his magic tricks so long that the people became his followers. 12 But Philip told them the Good News[d] about the kingdom of God and the power of Jesus Christ. Men and women believed Philip and were baptized. 13 Simon himself believed and was baptized. He stayed very close to Philip. When he saw the miracles and the very powerful things that Philip did, Simon was amazed.

14 The apostles[d] were still in Jerusalem. They heard that the people of Samaria had accepted the word of God. So they sent Peter and John to them.

15 When Peter and John arrived, they prayed that the Samaritan believers might receive the Holy Spirit.[d] 16 These people had been baptized in the name of the Lord Jesus. But the Holy Spirit had not yet entered any of them.

17 Then, when the two apostles began laying their hands on[n] the people, they received the Holy Spirit. 18 Simon saw that the Spirit was given to people when the apostles laid their hands on them. So he offered the apostles money. 19 He said,

"Give me also this power so that when I lay my hands on a person, he will receive the Holy Spirit."

20 Peter said to him,

"You and your money should both be destroyed! You thought you could buy God's gift with money. 21 You cannot share with us in this work. Your heart is not right before God."

8:17 laying their hands on Here, doing this showed that these men were given a special work of God.

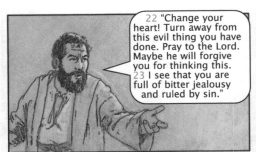

22 "Change your heart! Turn away from this evil thing you have done. Pray to the Lord. Maybe he will forgive you for thinking this. 23 I see that you are full of bitter jealousy and ruled by sin."

24 Simon answered,

"Both of you pray for me to the Lord. Pray that the things you have said will not happen to me!"

25 Then the two apostles told the people the things they had seen Jesus do. And after the apostles had given the message of the Lord, they went back to Jerusalem. On the way, they went through many Samaritan towns and preached the Good News to the people.

Philip Teaches an Ethiopian

26 An angel of the Lord spoke to Philip.ⁿ The angel said,

"Get ready and go south. Go to the road that leads down to Gaza from Jerusalem—the desert road."

27 So Philip got ready and went.

On the road he saw a man from Ethiopia, a eunuch.ᵈ He was an important officer in the service of Candace, the queen of the Ethiopians. He was responsible for taking care of all her money. He had gone to Jerusalem to worship, and

28 now he was on his way home. He was sitting in his chariot and reading from the book of Isaiah, the prophet.ᵈ

29 The Spiritᵈ said to Philip,

"Go to that chariot and stay near it."

8:26 **Philip** Not the apostle named Philip.

31

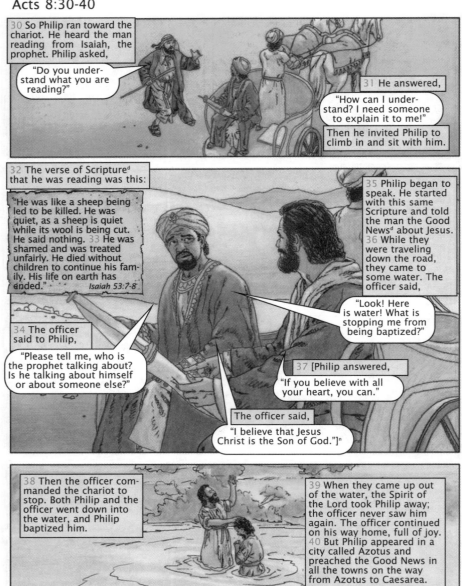

30 So Philip ran toward the chariot. He heard the man reading from Isaiah, the prophet. Philip asked,

"Do you understand what you are reading?"

31 He answered,

"How can I understand? I need someone to explain it to me!"

Then he invited Philip to climb in and sit with him.

32 The verse of Scripture[d] that he was reading was this:

"He was like a sheep being led to be killed. He was quiet, as a sheep is quiet while its wool is being cut. He said nothing. 33 He was shamed and was treated unfairly. He died without children to continue his family. His life on earth has ended."   Isaiah 53:7-8

34 The officer said to Philip,

"Please tell me, who is the prophet talking about? Is he talking about himself or about someone else?"

35 Philip began to speak. He started with this same Scripture and told the man the Good News[d] about Jesus. 36 While they were traveling down the road, they came to some water. The officer said,

"Look! Here is water! What is stopping me from being baptized?"

37 [Philip answered,

"If you believe with all your heart, you can."

The officer said,

"I believe that Jesus Christ is the Son of God."][n]

38 Then the officer commanded the chariot to stop. Both Philip and the officer went down into the water, and Philip baptized him.

39 When they came up out of the water, the Spirit of the Lord took Philip away; the officer never saw him again. The officer continued on his way home, full of joy. 40 But Philip appeared in a city called Azotus and preached the Good News in all the towns on the way from Azotus to Caesarea.

8:37 Philip . . . God. Some Greek copies do not contain the bracketed text.

Chapter 9

Saul Is Converted

1 In Jerusalem Saul was still trying to frighten the followers of the Lord by saying he would kill them. So he went to the high priest 2 and asked him to write letters to the synagogues^d in the city of Damascus. Saul wanted the high priest to give him the authority to find people in Damascus who were followers of Christ's Way. If he found any there, men or women, he would arrest them and bring them back to Jerusalem.

3 So Saul went to Damascus. As he came near the city, a bright light from heaven suddenly flashed around him. 4 Saul fell to the ground. He heard a voice saying to him,

"Saul, Saul! Why are you doing things against me?"

5 Saul said,

"Who are you, Lord?"

The voice answered,

"I am Jesus. I am the One you are trying to hurt. 6 Get up now and go into the city. Someone there will tell you what you must do."

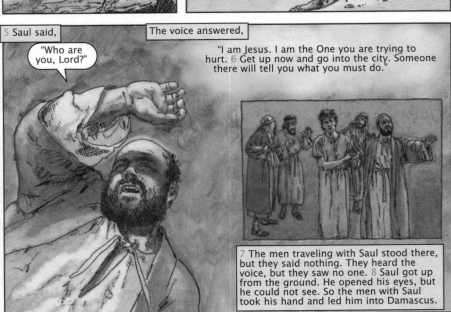

7 The men traveling with Saul stood there, but they said nothing. They heard the voice, but they saw no one. 8 Saul got up from the ground. He opened his eyes, but he could not see. So the men with Saul took his hand and led him into Damascus.

9 For three days Saul could not see, and he did not eat or drink.

10 There was a follower of Jesus in Damascus named Ananias. The Lord spoke to Ananias in a vision,

"Ananias!"

Ananias answered

"Here I am, Lord."

11 The Lord said to him,

"Get up and go to the street called Straight Street. Find the house of Judas." Ask for a man named Saul from the city of Tarsus. He is there now, praying. 12 Saul has seen a vision. In it a man named Ananias comes to him and lays his hands on him. Then he sees again."

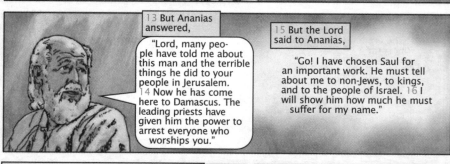

13 But Ananias answered,

"Lord, many people have told me about this man and the terrible things he did to your people in Jerusalem. 14 Now he has come here to Damascus. The leading priests have given him the power to arrest everyone who worships you."

15 But the Lord said to Ananias,

"Go! I have chosen Saul for an important work. He must tell about me to non-Jews, to kings, and to the people of Israel. 16 I will show him how much he must suffer for my name."

17 So Ananias went to the house of Judas.

He laid his hands on Saul and said,

"Brother Saul, the Lord Jesus sent me. He is the one you saw on the road on your way here. He sent me so that you can see again and be filled with the Holy Spirit."d

9:11 Judas This is not either of the apostles named Judas.

18 Immediately, something that looked like fish scales fell from Saul's eyes. He was able to see again!

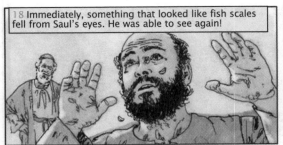

Then Saul got up and was baptized.

19 After eating some food, his strength returned.

Saul Preaches in Damascus

Saul stayed with the followers of Jesus in Damascus for a few days.

20 Soon he began to preach about Jesus in the synagogues,[d] saying,

"Jesus is the Son of God!"

21 All the people who heard him were amazed. They said,

"This is the man who was in Jerusalem. He was trying to destroy those who trust in this name! He came here to do the same thing. He came here to arrest the followers of Jesus and take them back to the leading priests."

22 But Saul became more and more powerful. His proofs that Jesus is the Christ[d] were so strong that the Jews in Damascus could not argue with him.

Saul Escapes from Damascus

23 After many days, the Jews made plans to kill Saul. 24 They were watching the city gates day and night. They wanted to kill him, but Saul learned about their plan.

25 One night some followers of Saul helped him leave the city. They lowered him in a basket through an opening in the city wall.

35

Saul in Jerusalem

26 Then Saul went to Jerusalem. He tried to join the group of followers, but they were all afraid of him. They did not believe that he was really a follower.

27 But Barnabas accepted Saul and took him to the apostles.[d] Barnabas told them that Saul had seen the Lord on the road. He explained how the Lord had spoken to Saul. Then he told them how boldly Saul had preached in the name of Jesus in Damascus.

28 And so Saul stayed with the followers. He went everywhere in Jerusalem, preaching boldly in the name of Jesus.

29 He would often talk and argue with the Jews who spoke Greek. But they were trying to kill him.

30 When the brothers learned about this, they took Saul to Caesarea. From there they sent him to Tarsus.

31 The church everywhere in Judea, Galilee, and Samaria had a time of peace. With the help of the Holy Spirit,[d] the group became stronger. The believers showed that they respected the Lord by the way they lived. Because of this, the group of believers grew larger and larger.

Peter Heals Aeneas

32 As Peter was traveling through all the area, he visited God's people who lived in Lydda.

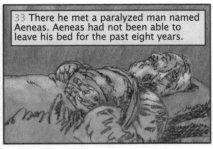

33 There he met a paralyzed man named Aeneas. Aeneas had not been able to leave his bed for the past eight years.

34 Peter said to him,

"Aeneas, Jesus Christ heals you. Stand up and make your bed!"

Aeneas stood up immediately. 35 All the people living in Lydda and on the Plain of Sharon saw him. These people turned to the Lord.

Peter in Joppa

36 In the city of Joppa there was a follower named Tabitha. (Her Greek name, Dorcas, means "a deer.") She was always doing good and helping the poor.

37 While Peter was in Lydda, Tabitha became sick and died. Her body was washed and put in a room upstairs.

Acts 9:38-41

38 The followers in Joppa heard that Peter was in Lydda. (Lydda is near Joppa.) So they sent two men to Peter. They begged him,

"Hurry, please come to us!"

39 Peter got ready and went with them. When he arrived, they took him to the upstairs room. All the widows stood around Peter, crying. They showed him the shirts and coats that Tabitha had made when she was still alive.

40 Peter sent everyone out of the room. He kneeled and prayed.

Then he turned to the body and said,

"Tabitha, stand up!"

She opened her eyes, and when she saw Peter, she sat up.

41 He gave her his hand and helped her up.

Then he called the saints[d] and the widows into the room. He showed them Tabitha; she was alive!

42 People everywhere in Joppa learned about this, and many believed in the Lord. 43 Peter stayed in Joppa for many days with a man named Simon who was a leatherworker.

Chapter **10**

Peter and Cornelius

1 At Caesarea there was a man named Cornelius. He was an officer in the Italian group of the Roman army.

2 Cornelius was a religious man. He and all the other people who lived in his house worshiped the true God. He gave much of his money to the poor and prayed to God often. 3 One afternoon about three o'clock, Cornelius saw a vision clearly. In the vision an angel of God came to him and said,

"Cornelius!"

4 Cornelius stared at the angel. He became afraid and said,

"What do you want, Lord?"

The angel said,

"God has heard your prayers. He has seen what you give to the poor. And God remembers you. 5 Send some men now to Joppa to bring back a man named Simon. Simon is also called Peter. 6 Simon is staying with a man, also named Simon, who is a leatherworker. He has a house beside the sea."

Acts 10:7-12

7 Then the angel who spoke to Cornelius left. Cornelius called two of his servants and a soldier. The soldier was a religious man who worked for Cornelius. 8 Cornelius explained everything to these three men and sent them to Joppa.

9 The next day as they came near Joppa, Peter was going up to the roof to pray. It was about noon. 10 Peter was hungry and wanted to eat. But while the food was being prepared, he had a vision. 11 He saw heaven opened and something coming down. It looked like a big sheet being lowered to earth by its four corners.

12 In it were all kinds of animals, reptiles, and birds.

10:9 roof In Bible times houses were built with flat roofs. The roof was used for drying things such as flax and fruit. And it was used as an extra room, as a place for worship and as a place to sleep in the summer.

40

13 Then a voice said to Peter,

"Get up, Peter; kill and eat!"

14 But Peter said,

"No, Lord! I have never eaten food that is unholy or unclean."[d]

15 But the voice said to him again,

"God has made these things clean. Don't call them 'unholy'!"

16 This happened three times. Then the sheet was taken back to heaven.
17 While Peter was wondering what this vision meant, the men Cornelius sent had found Simon's house. They were standing at the gate.

18 They asked,

"Is Simon Peter staying here?"

19 Peter was still thinking about the vision. But the Spirit[d] said to him,

"Listen! Three men are looking for you. 20 Get up and go downstairs. Go with them and don't ask questions. I have sent them to you."

21 So Peter went down to the men. He said,

"I am the man you are looking for. Why did you come here?"

22 They said,

"A holy angel spoke to Cornelius, an army officer. He is a good man; he worships God. All the Jewish people respect him. The angel told Cornelius to ask you to his house so that he can hear what you have to say."

23 Peter asked the men to come in and spend the night.

The next day Peter got ready and went with them. Some of the brothers from Joppa joined him. 24 On the following day they came to Caesarea.

Cornelius was waiting for them. He had called together his relatives and close friends. 25 When Peter entered, Cornelius met him. He fell at Peter's feet and worshiped him.

26 But Peter helped him up, saying,

"Stand up! I too am only a man."

27 Peter went on talking with Cornelius as they went inside. There Peter saw many people together.

28 He said,

"You people understand that it is against our Jewish law for a Jew to associate with or visit anyone who is not a Jew. But God has shown me that I should not call any person 'unholy' or 'unclean.'

29 That is why I did not argue when I was asked to come here. Now, please tell me why you sent for me."

30 Cornelius said,

"Four days ago, I was praying in my house. It was at this same time—three o'clock in the afternoon. Suddenly, there was a man standing before me wearing shining clothes.

31 He said, 'Cornelius! God has heard your prayer. He has seen what you give to the poor. And God remembers you. 32 So send some men to Joppa and ask Simon Peter to come. Peter is staying in the house of a man, also named Simon, who is a leatherworker. His house is beside the sea."

33 So I sent for you immediately, and it was very good of you to come. Now we are all here before God to hear everything the Lord has commanded you to tell us."

Acts 10:34-43

10:37 John John the Baptist, who preached to people about Christ's coming (Matthew 3, Luke 3).

Non-Jews Receive the Holy Spirit

44 While Peter was still saying this, the Holy Spirit[d] came down on all those who were listening. 45 The Jewish believers who came with Peter were amazed that the gift of the Holy Spirit had been given even to the non-Jewish people. 46 These Jewish believers heard them speaking in different languages and praising God. Then Peter said,

47 "Can anyone keep these people from being baptized with water? They have received the Holy Spirit just as we did!"

48 So Peter ordered that they be baptized in the name of Jesus Christ. Then they asked Peter to stay with them for a few days.

Chapter 11

Peter Returns to Jerusalem

1 The apostles[d] and the believers in Judea heard that non-Jewish people had accepted God's teaching too. 2 But when Peter came to Jerusalem, some Jewish believers argued with him. 3 They said,

"You went into the homes of people who are not Jews and are not circumcised![d] You even ate with them!"

4 So Peter explained the whole story to them. 5 He said,

"I was in the city of Joppa. While I was praying, I had a vision. In the vision, I saw something which looked like a big sheet coming down from heaven. It was being lowered to earth by its four corners. It came down very close to me, and 6 I looked inside it. I saw animals, wild beasts, reptiles, and birds.

7 "I heard a voice say to me, 'Get up, Peter. Kill and eat.'

8 But I said, 'No, Lord! I have never eaten anything that is unholy or unclean.'d 9 But the voice from heaven answered again, 'God has made these things clean. Don't call them unholy!' 10 This happened three times. Then the whole thing was taken back to heaven.

11 Right then three men came to the house where I was staying. They were sent to me from Caesarea.

12 The Spiritd told me to go with them without doubting. These six believers here also went with me. We went to the house of Cornelius.

13 He told us about the angel he saw standing in his house. The angel said to him, 'Send some men to Joppa and invite Simon Peter to come.

14 " 'He will speak to you. The things he will say will save you and all your family.'

15 When I began my speech, the Holy Spirit came on them just as he came on us at the beginning.

16 Then I remembered the words of the Lord. He said, 'John baptized in water, but you will be baptized in the Holy Spirit!' 17 God gave to them the same gift that he gave to us who believed in the Lord Jesus Christ. So could I stop the work of God? No!"

18 When the Jewish believers heard this, they stopped arguing. They praised God and said,

"So God is allowing the non-Jewish people also to turn to him and live."

Acts 11:19-30

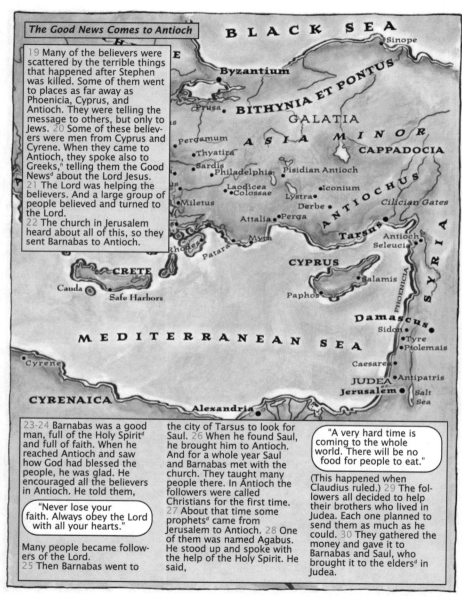

The Good News Comes to Antioch

19 Many of the believers were scattered by the terrible things that happened after Stephen was killed. Some of them went to places as far away as Phoenicia, Cyprus, and Antioch. They were telling the message to others, but only to Jews. 20 Some of these believers were men from Cyprus and Cyrene. When they came to Antioch, they spoke also to Greeks,[n] telling them the Good News about the Lord Jesus. 21 The Lord was helping the believers. And a large group of people believed and turned to the Lord. 22 The church in Jerusalem heard about all of this, so they sent Barnabas to Antioch.

23-24 Barnabas was a good man, full of the Holy Spirit[d] and full of faith. When he reached Antioch and saw how God had blessed the people, he was glad. He encouraged all the believers in Antioch. He told them,

"Never lose your faith. Always obey the Lord with all your hearts."

Many people became followers of the Lord. 25 Then Barnabas went to the city of Tarsus to look for Saul. 26 When he found Saul, he brought him to Antioch. And for a whole year Saul and Barnabas met with the church. They taught many people there. In Antioch the followers were called Christians for the first time. 27 About that time some prophets[d] came from Jerusalem to Antioch. 28 One of them was named Agabus. He stood up and spoke with the help of the Holy Spirit. He said,

"A very hard time is coming to the whole world. There will be no food for people to eat."

(This happened when Claudius ruled.) 29 The followers all decided to help their brothers who lived in Judea. Each one planned to send them as much as he could. 30 They gathered the money and gave it to Barnabas and Saul, who brought it to the elders[d] in Judea.

11:20 Greeks Some Greek copies read "Hellenists," non-Greeks who spoke Greek.

Chapter 12

Herod Agrippa Hurts the Church

1 During that same time King Herod began to do terrible things to some who belonged to the church. 2 He ordered James, the brother of John, to be killed by the sword.

3 Herod saw that the Jews liked this, so he decided to arrest Peter, too. (This happened during the time of the Feast[d] of Unleavened Bread.)

4 After Herod arrested Peter, he put him in jail and handed him over to be guarded by 16 soldiers. Herod planned to bring Peter before the people for trial after the Passover[d] Feast.

5 So Peter was kept in jail. But the church kept on praying to God for him.

Peter Leaves the Jail

6 The night before Herod was to bring him to trial, Peter was sleeping. He was between two soldiers, bound with two chains. Other soldiers were guarding the door of the jail.

Acts 12:7-11

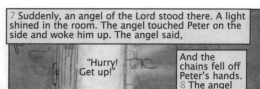

7 Suddenly, an angel of the Lord stood there. A light shined in the room. The angel touched Peter on the side and woke him up. The angel said,

"Hurry! Get up!"

And the chains fell off Peter's hands. 8 The angel said to him,

"Get dressed and put on your sandals."

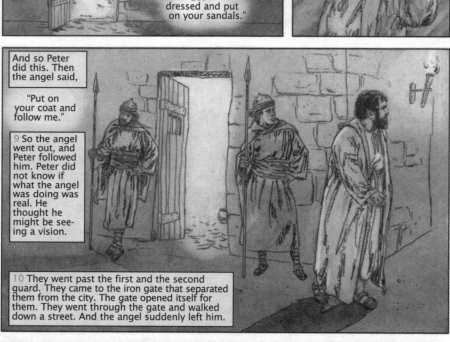

And so Peter did this. Then the angel said,

"Put on your coat and follow me."

9 So the angel went out, and Peter followed him. Peter did not know if what the angel was doing was real. He thought he might be seeing a vision.

10 They went past the first and the second guard. They came to the iron gate that separated them from the city. The gate opened itself for them. They went through the gate and walked down a street. And the angel suddenly left him.

11 Then Peter realized what had happened. He thought,

"Now I know that the Lord really sent his angel to me. He rescued me from Herod and from all the things the Jewish people thought would happen."

51

16 Peter continued to knock. When they opened the door, they saw him and were amazed.

17 Peter made a sign with his hand to tell them to be quiet. He explained how the Lord led him out of the jail. And he said,

"Tell James and the other believers what happened."

Then he left to go to another place.

18 The next day the soldiers were very upset. They wondered what had happened to Peter.

19 Herod looked everywhere for Peter but could not find him. So he questioned the guards and ordered that they be killed.

The Death of Herod Agrippa

Later Herod moved from Judea and went to the city of Caesarea, where he stayed for a while. 20 Herod was very angry with the people of Tyre and Sidon. But the people of those cities all came in a group to Herod. They were able to get Blastus, the king's personal servant, on their side. They asked Herod for peace because their country got its food from his country. 21 On a chosen day Herod put on his royal robes. He sat on his throne and made a speech to the people.

22 They shouted,

"This is the voice of a god, not a man!"

23 Herod did not give the glory to God. So an angel of the Lord caused him to become sick. He was eaten by worms and died.

24 God's message continued to spread and reach more and more people.
25 After Barnabas and Saul finished their task in Jerusalem, they returned to Antioch. John, also called Mark, was with them.

Chapter 13

1 In the church at Antioch there were these prophets[d] and teachers: Barnabas, Simeon (also called Niger), Lucius (from the city of Cyrene), Manaen (who had grown up with Herod, the ruler) and Saul. 2 They were all worshiping the Lord and giving up eating.[n] The Holy Spirit[d] said to them,

"Give Barnabas and Saul to me to do a special work. I have chosen them for it."

Barnabas and Saul Are Chosen

3 So they gave up eating and prayed. They laid their hands on[n] Barnabas and Saul and sent them out.

Barnabas and Saul in Cyprus

4 Barnabas and Saul were sent out by the Holy Spirit.[d]

13:2 giving up eating This is called "fasting." The people would give up eating for a special time of prayer and worship to God. It was also done to show sadness.
13:3 laid their hands on Here, this was a sign to show that these men were given a special work of God.

They went to the city of Seleucia. From there they sailed to the island of Cyprus.

5 When they came to Salamis, they preached the Good News[d] of God in the Jewish synagogues.[d] John Mark was with them to help. 6 They went across the whole island to Paphos.

In Paphos they met a Jew who was a magician. His name was Bar-Jesus. He was a false prophet,[d] 7 who always stayed close to Sergius Paulus, the governor. Sergius Paulus was a smart man.

He asked Barnabas and Saul to come to him, because he wanted to hear the message of God. 8 But Elymas, the magician, was against them. (Elymas is the name for Bar-Jesus in the Greek language.) He tried to stop the governor from believing in Jesus. 9 But Saul was filled with the Holy Spirit. (Saul's other name was Paul.) He looked straight at Elymas 10 and said,

"You son of the devil! You are an enemy of everything that is right! You are full of evil tricks and lies. You are always trying to change the Lord's truths into lies!

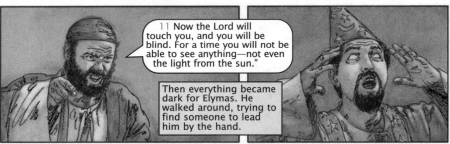

11 Now the Lord will touch you, and you will be blind. For a time you will not be able to see anything—not even the light from the sun."

Then everything became dark for Elymas. He walked around, trying to find someone to lead him by the hand.

12 When the governor saw this, he believed. He was amazed at the teaching about the Lord.

Paul and Barnabas Leave Cyprus

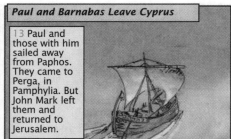

13 Paul and those with him sailed away from Paphos. They came to Perga, in Pamphylia. But John Mark left them and returned to Jerusalem.

14 They continued their trip from Perga and went to Antioch, a city in Pisidia.

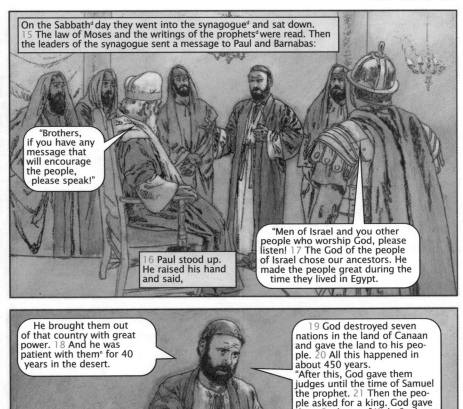

On the Sabbath[d] day they went into the synagogue[d] and sat down.
15 The law of Moses and the writings of the prophets[d] were read. Then the leaders of the synagogue sent a message to Paul and Barnabas:

"Brothers, if you have any message that will encourage the people, please speak!"

16 Paul stood up. He raised his hand and said,

"Men of Israel and you other people who worship God, please listen! 17 The God of the people of Israel chose our ancestors. He made the people great during the time they lived in Egypt.

He brought them out of that country with great power. 18 And he was patient with them[n] for 40 years in the desert.

19 God destroyed seven nations in the land of Canaan and gave the land to his people. 20 All this happened in about 450 years.
"After this, God gave them judges until the time of Samuel the prophet. 21 Then the people asked for a king. God gave them Saul son of Kish. Saul was from the tribe[d] of Benjamin. He was king for 40 years.

22 After God took him away, God made David their king. This is what God said about him: 'I have found David son of Jesse. He is the kind of man I want. He will do all that I want him to do.'

13:18 And . . . them Some Greek copies read "And he cared for them."

23 "So God has brought one of David's descendants[d] to Israel to be their Savior.[d] That descendant is Jesus. And God promised to do this. 24 Before Jesus came, John[n] preached to all the people of Israel. He told them about a baptism of changed hearts and lives.

25 When he was finishing his work, he said, 'Who do you think I am? I am not the Christ.[d] He is coming later. I am not worthy to untie his sandals.'

26 "Brothers, sons in the family of Abraham, and you non-Jews who worship God, listen! The news about this salvation has been sent to us. 27 Those who live in Jerusalem and their leaders did not realize that Jesus was the Savior. They did not understand the words that the prophets wrote, which are read every Sabbath[d] day. But they made them come true when they said Jesus was guilty.

28 They could not find any real reason for Jesus to die, but they asked Pilate to have him killed.

13:24 John John the Baptist, who preached to people about Christ's coming (Matthew 3, Luke 3).

29 "They did to him all that the Scriptures[d] had said. Then they took him down from the cross and laid him in a tomb.

30 But God raised him up from death!

31 After this, for many days, the people who had gone with Jesus from Galilee to Jerusalem saw him. They are now his witnesses to the people.

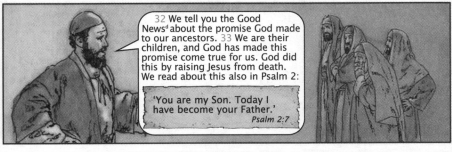

32 We tell you the Good News[d] about the promise God made to our ancestors. 33 We are their children, and God has made this promise come true for us. God did this by raising Jesus from death. We read about this also in Psalm 2:

'You are my Son. Today I have become your Father.'
Psalm 2:7

34 God raised Jesus from death. He will never go back to the grave and become dust. So God said:

'I will give you the holy and sure blessings that I promised to David.' Isaiah 55:3

35 But in another place God says:

'You will not let your Holy One rot in the grave.' Psalm 16:10

36 David did God's will during his lifetime. Then he died and was buried with his fathers. And his body did rot in the grave! 37 But the One God raised from death did not rot in the grave.

38-39 "Brothers, you must understand what we are telling you: You can have forgiveness of your sins through Jesus. The law of Moses could not free you from your sins. But everyone who believes is free from all sins through him. 40 Be careful! Don't let what the prophets said happen to you:

41 'Listen, you people who doubt! You can wonder, and then die. I will do something in your lifetime that will amaze you. You won't believe it even when you are told about it!' "

Habakkuk 1:5

42 While Paul and Barnabas were leaving the synagogue, the people asked them to tell them more about these things on the next Sabbath. 43 After the meeting, many Jews followed Paul and Barnabas from that place. With the Jews there were many who had changed to the Jewish religion and worshiped God. Paul and Barnabas were persuading them to continue trusting in God's kindness.

44 On the next Sabbath day, almost all the people in the city came to hear the word of the Lord.

45 Seeing the crowd, the Jews became very jealous. They said insulting things and argued against what Paul said. 46 But Paul and Barnabas spoke very boldly. They said,

"We must speak the message of God to you first. But you refuse to listen. You are judging yourselves not worthy of having eternal life! So we will now go to the people of other nations! 47 This is what the Lord told us to do. The Lord said:

'I have made you a light for the non-Jewish nations. You will show people all over the world the way to be saved.' "

Isaiah 49:6

48 When the non-Jewish people heard Paul say this, they were happy. They gave honor to the message of the Lord. And many of the people believed the message. They were the ones chosen to have life forever.

49 And so the message of the Lord was spreading through the whole country. 50 But the Jews stirred up some of the important religious women and the leaders of the city against Paul and Barnabas. They started trouble against Paul and Barnabas and drove them out of their area.

51 So Paul and Barnabas shook the dust off their feet[n] and went to Iconium. 52 But the followers were filled with joy and the Holy Spirit.[d]

13:51 shook . . . feet A warning. It showed that they were finished talking to these people.

Chapter 14

Paul and Barnabas in Iconium

1 In Iconium, Paul and Barnabas went as usual to the Jewish synagogue.[d] They spoke so well that a great many Jews and Greeks believed.

2 But some of the Jews who did not believe excited the non-Jewish people and turned them against the believers.

3 But Paul and Barnabas stayed in Iconium a long time and spoke bravely for the Lord. The Lord showed that their message about his grace was true by giving them the power to work miracles[d] and signs.

4 But some of the people in the city agreed with the Jews. Others believed the apostles.d So the city was divided.

5 Some non-Jewish people, some Jews, and some of their rulers wanted to harm Paul and Barnabas by killing them with stones. 6 When Paul and Barnabas learned about this, they went to Lystra and Derbe, cities in Lycaonia, and to the areas around those cities. 7 They announced the Good Newsd there, too.

Paul in Lystra and Derbe

8 In Lystra there sat a man who had been born crippled; he had never walked.

9 This man was listening to Paul speak. Paul looked straight at him and saw that the man believed God could heal him. 10 So he cried out,

"Stand up on your feet!"

The man jumped up and began walking around.

11 When the crowds saw what Paul did, they shouted in their own Lycaonian language. They said,

"The gods have become like men! They have come down to us!"

12 And the people began to call Barnabas "Zeus."[n] They called Paul "Hermes,"[n] because he was the main speaker.

13 The temple of Zeus was near the city. The priest of this temple brought some bulls and flowers to the city gates. The priest and the people wanted to offer a sacrifice to Paul and Barnabas. 14 But when the apostles,[d] Barnabas and Paul, understood what they were about to do, they tore their clothes in anger.

14:12 "Zeus" The Greeks believed in many gods. Zeus was their most important god.
14:12 "Hermes" The Greeks believed he was a messenger for the other gods.

Then they ran in among the people and shouted,

15 "Men, why are you doing these things? We are only men, human beings like you! We are bringing you the Good News.ᵈ We are telling you to turn away from these worthless things and turn to the true living God. He is the One who made the sky, the earth, the sea, and everything that is in them. 16 In the past, God let all the nations do what they wanted.

17 Yet he did things to prove he is real: He shows kindness to you. He gives you rain from heaven and crops at the right times. He gives you food and fills your hearts with joy."

18 Even with these words, they were barely able to keep the crowd from offering sacrifices to them.

19 Then some Jews came from Antioch and Iconium. They persuaded the people to turn against Paul. And so they threw stones at Paul and dragged him out of town. They thought that they had killed him.

20 But the followers gathered around him, and he got up and went back into the town. The next day, he and Barnabas left and went to the city of Derbe.

Acts 14:21-28

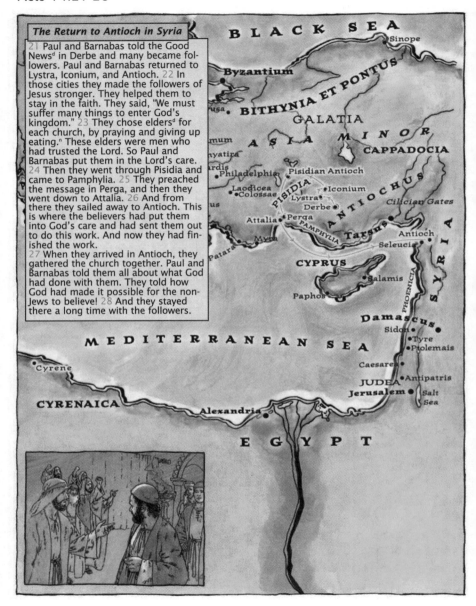

The Return to Antioch in Syria

21 Paul and Barnabas told the Good News[d] in Derbe and many became followers. Paul and Barnabas returned to Lystra, Iconium, and Antioch. 22 In those cities they made the followers of Jesus stronger. They helped them to stay in the faith. They said, "We must suffer many things to enter God's kingdom." 23 They chose elders[d] for each church, by praying and giving up eating.[n] These elders were men who had trusted the Lord. So Paul and Barnabas put them in the Lord's care. 24 Then they went through Pisidia and came to Pamphylia. 25 They preached the message in Perga, and then they went down to Attalia. 26 And from there they sailed away to Antioch. This is where the believers had put them into God's care and had sent them out to do this work. And now they had finished the work.
27 When they arrived in Antioch, they gathered the church together. Paul and Barnabas told them all about what God had done with them. They told how God had made it possible for the non-Jews to believe! 28 And they stayed there a long time with the followers.

14:23 giving up eating This is called "fasting." The people would give up eating for a special time of prayer and worship to God. It was also done to show sadness.

Chapter
15

The Meeting at Jerusalem

1 Then some men came to Antioch from Judea. They began teaching the non-Jewish brothers:

"You cannot be saved if you are not circumcised.[d] Moses taught us to do this."

2 Paul and Barnabas were against this teaching and argued with the men about it. So the group decided to send Paul, Barnabas, and some other men to Jerusalem. There they could talk more about this with the apostles[d] and elders.[d]

3 The church helped the men leave on the trip. They went through the countries of Phoenicia and Samaria, telling all about how the non-Jewish people had turned to God. This made all the believers very happy.

4 When they arrived in Jerusalem, the apostles, the elders, and the church welcomed them. Paul, Barnabas, and the others told about all the things that God had done with them.

5 But some of the believers who had belonged to the Pharisee[d] group came forward. They said,

"The non-Jewish believers must be circumcised. We must tell them to obey the law of Moses!"

6 The apostles and the elders gathered to study this problem.
7 There was a long debate. Then Peter stood up and said to them,

"Brothers, you know what happened in the early days. God chose me from among you to preach the Good News[d] to the non-Jewish people. They heard the Good News from me, and they believed.

8 God, who knows the thoughts of all men, accepted them. He showed this to us by giving them the Holy Spirit,[d] just as he did to us. 9 To God, those people are not different from us. When they believed, he made their hearts pure.

10 So now why are you testing God? You are putting a heavy load around the necks of the non-Jewish brothers. It is a load that neither we nor our fathers were able to carry.

11 But we believe that we and they too will be saved by the grace of the Lord Jesus!"

12 Then the whole group became quiet. They listened to Paul and Barnabas speak. Paul and Barnabas told about all the miracles[d] and signs that God did through them among the non-Jewish people.

13 After they finished speaking, James spoke. He said,

14 Simon has told us how God showed his love for the non-Jewish people. For the first time he has accepted them and made them his people. 15 The words of the prophets[d] agree with this too:

"Brothers, listen to me.

16 'After these things I will return. The kingdom of David is like a fallen tent. But I will rebuild it. And I will again build its ruins. And I will set it up. 17 Then those people who are left alive may ask the Lord for help. And all people from other nations may worship me, says the Lord. And he will make it happen. 18 And these things have been known for a long time.' *Amos 9:11-12*

19 "So I think we should not bother the non-Jewish brothers who have turned to God.

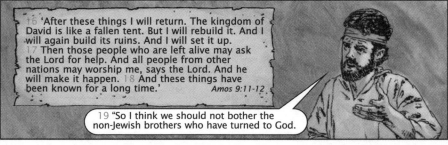

20 Instead, we should write a letter to them. We should tell them these things: Do not eat food that has been offered to idols. (This makes the food unclean.[d]) Do not take part in any kind of sexual sin. Do not taste blood. Do not eat animals that have been strangled. 21 They should not do these things, because there are still men in every city who teach the law of Moses. For a long time the words of Moses have been read in the synagogue[d] every Sabbath[d] day."

Letter to Non-Jewish Believers

22 The apostles,[d] the elders,[d] and the whole church decided to send some of their men with Paul and Barnabas to Antioch. They chose Judas Barsabbas and Silas, who were respected by the believers. 23 They sent the following letter with them:

From the apostles and elders, your brothers.

To all the non-Jewish brothers in Antioch, Syria and Cilicia:

Dear Brothers,

24 We have heard that some of our men have come to you and said things that trouble and upset you. But we did not tell them to do this! 25 We have all agreed to choose some men and send them to you. They will be with our dear friends Barnabas and Paul— 26 men who have given their lives to serve our Lord Jesus Christ. 27 So we have sent Judas and Silas with them. They will tell you the same things. 28 It has pleased the Holy Spirit[d] that you should not have a heavy load to carry, and we agree. You need to do only these things: 29 Do not eat any food that has been offered to idols. Do not taste blood. Do not eat any animals that have been strangled. Do not take part in any kind of sexual sin. If you stay away from these things, you will do well.

Good-bye.

30 So the men left Jerusalem and went to Antioch. There they gathered the church and gave them the letter.

31 When they read it, they were very happy because of the encouraging letter. 32 Judas and Silas were also prophets,[d] who said many things to encourage the believers and make them stronger.

33 After some time Judas and Silas were sent off in peace by the believers. They went back to those who had sent them.

34 [But Silas decided to remain there.]ⁿ 35 But Paul and Barnabas stayed in Antioch. They and many others preached the Good Newsᵈ and taught the people the message of the Lord.

Paul and Barnabas Separate

36 After some time, Paul said to Barnabas,

"We preached the message of the Lord in many towns. We should go back to all those towns to visit the believers and see how they are doing."

37 Barnabas wanted to take John Mark with them too.

38 But John Mark had left them at Pamphylia; he did not continue with them in the work. So Paul did not think it was a good idea to take him. 39 Paul and Barnabas had a serious argument about this. They separated and went different ways.

Barnabas sailed to Cyprus and took Mark with him.

40 But Paul chose Silas and left. The believers in Antioch put Paul into the Lord's care. 41 And he went through Syria and Cilicia, giving strength to the churches.

15:34 But . . . there. Some Greek copies do not contain the bracketed text.

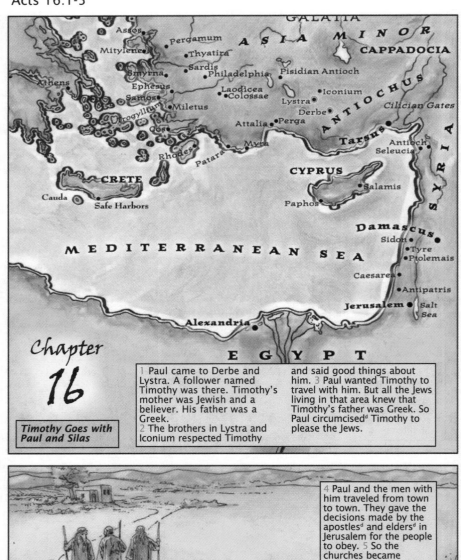

GALATIA

ASIA MINOR

CAPPADOCIA

Assos
Pergamum
Mitylene
Thyatira
Smyrna
Sardis
Pisidian Antioch
Ephesus
Philadelphia
Athens
Samos
Laodicea
Colossae
Iconium
ANTIOCHUS
Miletus
Lystra
Derbe
Cilician Gates
Trogyllium
Cos
Attalia
Perga
Tarsus
Rhodes
Myra
Antioch
Patara
Seleucia
CRETE
CYPRUS
SYRIA
Cauda
Safe Harbors
Salamis
Paphos
Damascus
MEDITERRANEAN SEA
Sidon
Tyre
Ptolemais
Caesarea
Antipatris
Jerusalem
Salt Sea
Alexandria
EGYPT

Chapter

16

Timothy Goes with Paul and Silas

1 Paul came to Derbe and Lystra. A follower named Timothy was there. Timothy's mother was Jewish and a believer. His father was a Greek.
2 The brothers in Lystra and Iconium respected Timothy and said good things about him. 3 Paul wanted Timothy to travel with him. But all the Jews living in that area knew that Timothy's father was Greek. So Paul circumcised[d] Timothy to please the Jews.

4 Paul and the men with him traveled from town to town. They gave the decisions made by the apostles[d] and elders[d] in Jerusalem for the people to obey. 5 So the churches became stronger in the faith and grew larger every day.

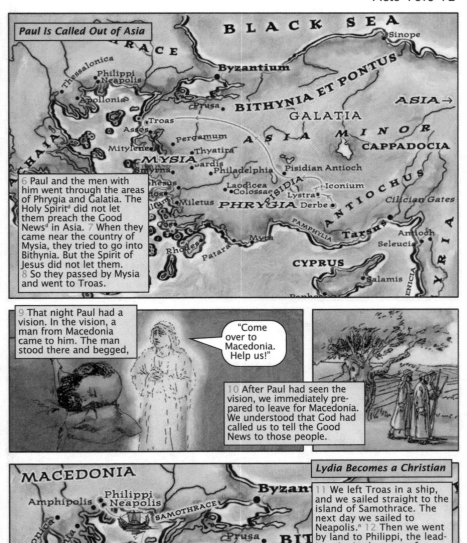

Paul Is Called Out of Asia

6 Paul and the men with him went through the areas of Phrygia and Galatia. The Holy Spirit[d] did not let them preach the Good News[d] in Asia. 7 When they came near the country of Mysia, they tried to go into Bithynia. But the Spirit of Jesus did not let them. 8 So they passed by Mysia and went to Troas.

9 That night Paul had a vision. In the vision, a man from Macedonia came to him. The man stood there and begged,

"Come over to Macedonia. Help us!"

10 After Paul had seen the vision, we immediately prepared to leave for Macedonia. We understood that God had called us to tell the Good News to those people.

Lydia Becomes a Christian

11 We left Troas in a ship, and we sailed straight to the island of Samothrace. The next day we sailed to Neapolis.[n] 12 Then we went by land to Philippi, the leading city in that part of Macedonia. It is also a Roman colony.[n] We stayed there for several days.

16:11 Neapolis City in Macedonia. It was the first city Paul visited on the continent of Europe. **16:12 Roman colony** A town begun by Romans with Roman laws, customs and privileges.

13 On the Sabbath[d] day we went outside the city gate to the river. There we thought we would find a special place for prayer. Some women had gathered there, so we sat down and talked with them.

14 There was a woman named Lydia from the city of Thyatira. Her job was selling purple cloth. She worshiped the true God. The Lord opened her mind to pay attention to what Paul was saying. 15 She and all the people in her house were baptized. Then Lydia invited us to her home. She said,

"If you think I am truly a believer in the Lord, then come stay in my house."

And she persuaded us to stay with her.

Paul and Silas in Jail

16 Once, while we were going to the place for prayer, a servant girl met us. She had a special spirit* in her. She earned a lot of money for her owners by telling fortunes.

17 This girl followed Paul and us. She said loudly,

"These men are servants of the Most High God! They are telling you how you can be saved!"

"By the power of Jesus Christ, I command you to come out of her!"

18 She kept this up for many days. This bothered Paul, so he turned and said to the spirit,

19 The owners of the servant girl saw this. These men knew that now they could not use her to make money. So they grabbed Paul and Silas and dragged them before the city rulers in the marketplace.

16:16 spirit This was a spirit from the devil. It caused her to say she had special knowledge.

Acts 16:20-24

20 Here they brought Paul and Silas to the Roman rulers and said,

"These men are Jews and are making trouble in our city. 21 They are teaching things that are not right for us as Romans to do."

22 The crowd joined the attack against them. The Roman officers tore the clothes of Paul and Silas and had them beaten with rods again and again.

23 Then Paul and Silas were thrown into jail. The jailer was ordered to guard them carefully. 24 When he heard this order, he put them far inside the jail. He pinned down their feet between large blocks of wood.

25 About midnight Paul and Silas were praying and singing songs to God. The other prisoners were listening to them. 26 Suddenly, there was a big earthquake. It was so strong that it shook the foundation of the jail.

Then all the doors of the jail broke open. All the prisoners were freed from their chains.

27 The jailer woke up and saw that the jail doors were open. He thought that the prisoners had already escaped. So he got his sword and was about to kill himself.ⁿ

28 But Paul shouted,

16:27 kill himself He thought the leaders would kill him for letting the prisoners escape.

"Don't hurt yourself! We are all here!"

29 The jailer told someone to bring a light. Then he ran inside. Shaking with fear, he fell down before Paul and Silas. 30 Then he brought them outside and said,

"Men, what must I do to be saved?"

31 They said to him,

"Believe in the Lord Jesus and you will be saved—you and all the people in your house."

32 So Paul and Silas told the message of the Lord to the jailer and all the people in his house. 33 At that hour of the night the jailer took Paul and Silas and washed their wounds. Then he and all his people were baptized immediately. 34 After this the jailer took Paul and Silas home and gave them food. He and his family were very happy because they now believed in God.

35 The next morning, the Roman officers sent the police to tell the jailer,

"Let these men go free!"

36 The jailer said to Paul,

"The officers have sent an order to let you go free. You can leave now. Go in peace."

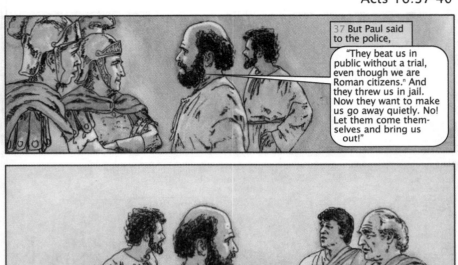

37 But Paul said to the police,

"They beat us in public without a trial, even though we are Roman citizens." And they threw us in jail. Now they want to make us go away quietly. No! Let them come themselves and bring us out!"

38 The police told the Roman officers what Paul said. When the officers heard that Paul and Silas were Roman citizens, they were afraid. 39 So they came and told Paul and Silas they were sorry. They took Paul and Silas out of jail and asked them to leave the city.

40 So when they came out of the jail, they went to Lydia's house. There they saw some of the believers and encouraged them. Then they left.

16:37 **Roman citizens** Roman law said that Roman citizens must not be beaten before they had a trial.

Acts 17:1-5

Chapter
17

Paul and Silas in Thessalonica

MACEDONIA

Amphipolis • Philippi • Neapolis

Thessalonica •

• Apollonia

Aegean Sea

Assos

1 Paul and Silas traveled through Amphipolis and Apollonia and came to Thessalonica. In that city there was a Jewish synagogue.[d]

2 Paul went into the synagogue as he always did. On each Sabbath[d] day for three weeks, Paul talked with the Jews about the Scriptures.[d]

3 He explained and proved that the Christ[d] must die and then rise from death. He said,

"This Jesus I am telling you about is the Christ."

4 Some of the Jews were convinced and joined Paul and Silas. Many of the Greeks who worshiped the true God and many of the important women joined them.

5 But the Jews became jealous. They got some evil men from the marketplace, formed a mob and started a riot.

They ran to Jason's house, looking for Paul and Silas. The men wanted to bring Paul and Silas out to the people. 6 But they did not find them. So they dragged Jason and some other believers to the leaders of the city. The people were yelling,

"These men have made trouble everywhere in the world. And now they have come here too! 7 Jason is keeping them in his house. All of them do things against the laws of Caesar.[d] They say that there is another king called Jesus."

8 When the people and the leaders of the city heard these things, they became very upset. 9 They made Jason and the others put up a sum of money. Then they let the believers go free.

Paul and Silas Go to Berea

10 That same night the believers sent Paul and Silas to Berea.

There Paul and Silas went to the Jewish synagogue.[d]

Acts 17:11-15

11 These Jews were better than the Jews in Thessalonica. They were eager to hear the things Paul and Silas said. These Jews in Berea studied the Scriptures[d] every day to find out if these things were true. 12 So, many of them believed. Many important Greek men and women also believed.

13 But when the Jews in Thessalonica learned that Paul was preaching the word of God in Berea, they came there, too. They upset the people and made trouble.

14 So the believers quickly sent Paul away to the coast. But Silas and Timothy stayed in Berea. 15 The men who took Paul went with him to Athens. Then they carried a message from Paul back to Silas and Timothy. It said, "Come to me as soon as you can."

Paul in Athens

16 Paul was waiting for Silas and Timothy in Athens. He was troubled because he saw that the city was full of idols.

17 In the synagogue,[d] he talked with the Jews and the Greeks who worshiped the true God.

He also talked every day with people in the marketplace.

18 Some of the Epicurean and Stoic philosophers[n] argued with him. Some of them said,

"This man doesn't know what he is talking about. What is he trying to say?"

Paul was telling them the Good News[d] of Jesus' rising from death.

They said,

"He seems to be telling us about some other gods."

17:18 Epicurean and Stoic philosophers Philosophers were those who searched for truth. Epicureans believed that pleasure, especially pleasures of the mind, were the goal of life. Stoics believed that life should be without feelings of joy or grief.

19 They got Paul and took him to a meeting of the Areopagus.[n] They said,

"Please explain to us this new idea that you have been teaching. 20 The things you are saying are new to us. We want to know what this teaching means."

21 (All the people of Athens and those from other countries always used their time talking about all the newest ideas.)
22 Then Paul stood before the meeting of the Areopagus. He said,

"Men of Athens, I can see that you are very religious in all things. 23 I was going through your city, and I saw the things you worship. I found an altar that had these words written on it: "TO A GOD WHO IS NOT KNOWN." You worship a god that you don't know. This is the God I am telling you about!

24 He is the God who made the whole world and everything in it. He is the Lord of the land and the sky. He does not live in temples that men build! 25 This God is the One who gives life, breath, and everything else to people. He does not need any help from them. He has everything he needs.

26 God began by making one man. From him came all the different people who live everywhere in the world. He decided exactly when and where they must live. 27 God wanted them to look for him and perhaps search all around for him and find him. But he is not far from any of us:

17:19 Areopagus A council or group of important leaders in Athens. They were like judges.

28 "'By his power we live and move and exist.' Some of your own poets have said: 'For we are his children.' 29 We are God's children. So, you must not think that God is like something that people imagine or make. He is not like gold, silver, or rock.

30 In the past, people did not understand God, but God ignored this. But now, God tells everyone in the world to change his heart and life.

31 God has decided on a day that he will judge all the world. He will be fair. He will use a man to do this. God chose that man long ago. And God has proved this to everyone by raising that man from death!"

32 When the people heard about Jesus being raised from death, some of them laughed. They said,

"We will hear more about this from you later."

33 So Paul went away from them. 34 But some of the people believed Paul and joined him. One of those who believed was Dionysius, a member of the Areopagus. Also a woman named Damaris and some others believed.

Chapter

18

Paul in Corinth

1 Later, Paul left Athens and went to Corinth.

2 Here he met a Jew named Aquila. Aquila was born in the country of Pontus. But Aquila and his wife, Priscilla, had recently moved to Corinth from Italy. They left Italy because Claudius[n] commanded that all Jews must leave Rome. Paul went to visit Aquila and Priscilla.

3 They were tentmakers, just as he was. He stayed with them and worked with them.

4 Every Sabbath[d] day he talked with the Jews and Greeks in the synagogue.[d] Paul tried to persuade these people to believe in Jesus.

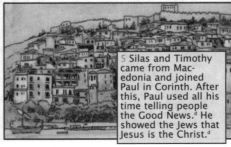

5 Silas and Timothy came from Macedonia and joined Paul in Corinth. After this, Paul used all his time telling people the Good News.[d] He showed the Jews that Jesus is the Christ.[d]

18:2 Claudius The emperor (ruler) of Rome, A.D. 41-54.

6 But they would not accept Paul's teaching and said some evil things. So he shook off the dust from his clothes.[n] He said to them,

"If you are not saved, it will be your own fault! I have done all I can do! After this, I will go to non-Jewish people!"

7 Paul left the synagogue and moved into the home of Titius Justus. It was next to the synagogue. This man worshiped the true God.

8 Crispus was the leader of that synagogue. He and all the people living in his house believed in the Lord. Many others in Corinth also listened to Paul. They too believed and were baptized.

9 During the night, Paul had a vision. The Lord said to him,

"Don't be afraid! Continue talking to people and don't be quiet! 10 I am with you. No one will hurt you because many of my people are in this city."

11 Paul stayed there for a year and a half, teaching God's word to the people.

18:6 shook . . . clothes This was a warning. It showed that Paul was finished talking to the Jews.

Paul Is Brought Before Gallio

12 Gallio became the governor of the country of Southern Greece. At that time, some of the Jews came together against Paul and took him to the court. 13 They said to Gallio,

"This man is teaching people to worship God in a way that is against our law!"

14 Paul was about to say something, but Gallio spoke to the Jews. Gallio said,

"I would listen to you Jews if you were complaining about a crime or some wrong. 15 But the things you are saying are only questions about words and names—arguments about your own law. So you must solve this problem yourselves. I don't want to be a judge of these things!"

16 Then Gallio made them leave the court.

17 Then they all grabbed Sosthenes. (Sosthenes was now the leader of the synagogue.ᵈ) They beat him there before the court. But this did not bother Gallio.

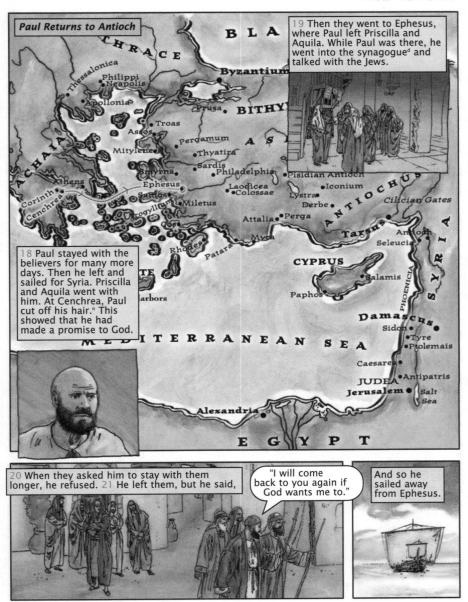

Paul Returns to Antioch

19 Then they went to Ephesus, where Paul left Priscilla and Aquila. While Paul was there, he went into the synagogue[d] and talked with the Jews.

18 Paul stayed with the believers for many more days. Then he left and sailed for Syria. Priscilla and Aquila went with him. At Cenchrea, Paul cut off his hair.[n] This showed that he had made a promise to God.

20 When they asked him to stay with them longer, he refused. 21 He left them, but he said,

"I will come back to you again if God wants me to."

And so he sailed away from Ephesus.

18:18 cut . . . hair Jews did this to show that the time of a special promise to God was finished.

Acts 18:22-27

22 Paul landed at Caesarea. Then he went and gave greetings to the church in Jerusalem. After that, Paul went to Antioch.

23 He stayed there for a while and then left and went through the countries of Galatia and Phrygia. He traveled from town to town in these countries, giving strength to all the followers.

Apollos in Ephesus and Corinth

24 A Jew named Apollos came to Ephesus. He was born in the city of Alexandria. He was an educated man who knew the Scriptures[d] well.

25 He had been taught about the Lord. He was always very excited when he spoke and taught the truth about Jesus. But the only baptism that Apollos knew about was the baptism that John[n] taught. 26 Apollos began to speak very boldly in the synagogue.[d] and Priscilla and Aquila heard him.

So they took him to their home and helped him better understand the way of God.

27 Now Apollos wanted to go to the country of Southern Greece, so the believers helped him. They wrote a letter to the followers there, asking them to accept him. These followers had believed in Jesus because of God's grace. When Apollos went there, he helped them very much.

18:25 John John the Baptist, who preached to people about Christ's coming (Matthew 3, Luke 3).

28 He argued very strongly with the Jews before all the people. Apollos clearly proved that the Jews were wrong. Using the Scriptures, he proved that Jesus is the Christ.[d]

Chapter 19

Paul in Ephesus

1 While Apollos was in Corinth, Paul was visiting some places on the way to Ephesus. There he found some followers.

2 Paul asked them,

"Did you receive the Holy Spirit[d] when you believed?"

They said,

"We have never even heard of a Holy Spirit!"

3 So he asked,

"What kind of baptism did you have?"

They said,

"It was the baptism that John[n] taught."

4 Paul said,

"John's baptism was a baptism of changed hearts and lives. He told people to believe in the One who would come after him. That One is Jesus."

5 When they heard this, they were baptized in the name of the Lord Jesus.

6 Then Paul laid his hands on them,[n] and the Holy Spirit came upon them. They began speaking different languages and prophesying.[d]
7 There were about 12 men in this group.

19:3 John John the Baptist, who preached to people about Christ's coming (Matthew 3, Luke 3). **19:6 laid his hands on them** Here, doing this was a sign to show that Paul had God's authority or power to give these people special powers of the Holy Spirit.

8 Paul went into the synagogue[d] and spoke out boldly for three months. He talked with the Jews and persuaded them to accept the things he said about the kingdom of God.

9 But some of the Jews became stubborn and refused to believe. These Jews said evil things about the Way of Jesus. All the people heard these things.

So Paul left them and took the followers with him. He went to a place where a man named Tyrannus had a school. There Paul talked with people every day

10 for two years. Because of his work, every Jew and Greek in Asia heard the word of the Lord.

The Sons of Sceva

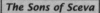

11 God used Paul to do some very special miracles.[d] 12 Some people took handkerchiefs and clothes that Paul had used and put them on the sick. When they did this, the sick were healed and evil spirits left them.

13-14 But some Jews also were traveling around and making evil spirits go out of people. The seven sons of Sceva were doing this. (Sceva was a leading Jewish priest.) These Jews tried to use the name of the Lord Jesus to force the evil spirits out. They would say,

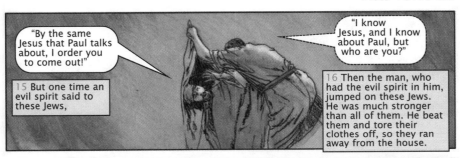

"By the same Jesus that Paul talks about, I order you to come out!"

"I know Jesus, and I know about Paul, but who are you?"

15 But one time an evil spirit said to these Jews,

16 Then the man, who had the evil spirit in him, jumped on these Jews. He was much stronger than all of them. He beat them and tore their clothes off, so they ran away from the house.

17 All the people in Ephesus, Jews and Greeks, learned about this. They were filled with fear. And the people gave great honor to the Lord Jesus. 18 Many of the believers began to confess openly and tell all the evil things they had done.

19 Some of them had used magic. These believers brought their magic books and burned them before everyone. Those books were worth about 50,000 silver coins."

20 So in a powerful way the word of the Lord kept spreading and growing.

19:19 50,000 silver coins Probably drachmas. One coin was enough to pay a man for working one day.

Acts 19:21-26

Paul Plans a Trip

21 After these things, Paul made plans to go to Jerusalem. He planned to go through the countries of Macedonia and Southern Greece, and then on to Jerusalem. He said,

"After I have been to Jerusalem, I must also visit Rome."

22 Paul sent Timothy and Erastus, two of his helpers, ahead to Macedonia. He himself stayed in Asia for a while.

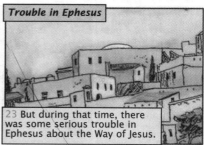

Trouble in Ephesus

23 But during that time, there was some serious trouble in Ephesus about the Way of Jesus.

24 There was a man named Demetrius, who worked with silver. He made little silver models that looked like the temple of the goddess Artemis." The men who did this work made much money. 25 Demetrius had a meeting with these men and some others who did the same kind of work. He told them,

"Men, you know that we make a lot of money from our business. 26 But look at what this man Paul is doing! He has convinced and turned away many people in Ephesus and in almost all of Asia! He says the gods that men make are not real."

19:24 Artemis A Greek goddess that the people of Asia Minor worshiped.

27 "There is a danger that our business will lose its good name. But there is also another danger: People will begin to think that the temple of the great goddess Artemis is not important! Her greatness will be destroyed. And Artemis is the goddess that everyone in Asia and the whole world worships."

28 When the men heard this, they became very angry. They shouted,

"Artemis, the goddess of Ephesus, is great!"

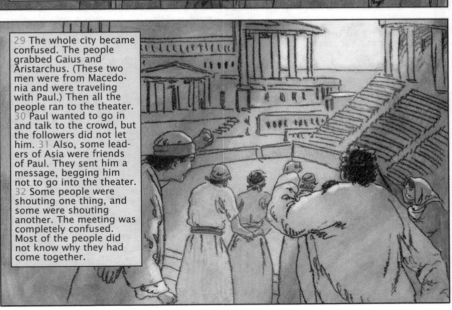

29 The whole city became confused. The people grabbed Gaius and Aristarchus. (These two men were from Macedonia and were traveling with Paul.) Then all the people ran to the theater. 30 Paul wanted to go in and talk to the crowd, but the followers did not let him. 31 Also, some leaders of Asia were friends of Paul. They sent him a message, begging him not to go into the theater. 32 Some people were shouting one thing, and some were shouting another. The meeting was completely confused. Most of the people did not know why they had come together.

"Great is Artemis of Ephesus!"

33 The Jews put a man named Alexander in front of the people. Some of them had told him what to do. Alexander waved his hand because he wanted to explain things to the people. 34 But when they saw that Alexander was a Jew, they all began shouting the same thing. They continued shouting for two hours:

35 Then the city clerk made the crowd be quiet. He said,

"Men of Ephesus, everyone knows that Ephesus is the city that keeps the temple of the great goddess Artemis. All people know that we also keep her holy stone[n] that fell from heaven. 36 No one can say that this is not true. So you should be quiet. You must stop and think before you do anything. 37 You brought these men here, but they have not said anything evil against our goddess. They have not stolen anything from her temple. 38 We have courts of law, and there are judges. Do Demetrius and the men who work with him have a charge against anyone? They should go to the courts! That is where they can argue with each other! 39 Is there something else you want to talk about? It can be decided at the regular town meeting of the people.

19:35 holy stone Probably a meteorite or stone that the people thought looked like Artemis.

40 "I say this because some people might see this trouble today and say that we are rioting. We could not explain this because there is no real reason for this meeting."

41 After the city clerk said these things, he told the people to go home.

Chapter 20

Paul in Macedonia and Greece

1 When the trouble stopped, Paul sent for the followers to come to him. He encouraged them and then told them good-bye.

Paul left and went to the country of Macedonia. 2 He said many things to strengthen the followers in the different places on his way through Macedonia. Then he went to Southern Greece. 3 He stayed there three months. He was ready to sail for Syria, but some Jews were planning something against him. So Paul decided to go back through Macedonia to Syria.

Acts 20:4-9

4 Some men went with him. They were Sopater son of Pyrrhus, from the city of Berea; Aristarchus and Secundus, from the city of Thessalonica; Gaius, from Derbe; and Timothy; and Tychicus and Trophimus, two men from Asia.

5 These men went first, ahead of Paul, and waited for us at Troas. 6 We sailed from Philippi after the Feast[d] of Unleavened Bread and we met them in Troas five days later. We stayed there seven days.

Paul's Last Visit to Troas

7 On the first day of the week,[n] we all met together to break bread.[n] Paul spoke to the group. Because he was planning to leave the next day, he kept on talking till midnight. 8 We were all together in a room upstairs, and there were many lamps in the room. 9 A young man named Eutychus was sitting in the window. As Paul continued talking, Eutychus was falling into a deep sleep.

20:7 first day of the week Sunday, which for the Jews began at sunset on our Saturday. But if in this part of Asia a different system of time was used, then the meeting was on our Sunday night. **20:7 break bread** Probably the Lord's Supper, the special meal that Jesus told his followers to eat to remember him (Luke 22:14-20).

Finally, he went sound asleep and fell to the ground from the third floor. When they picked him up, he was dead.

10 Paul went down to Eutychus. He knelt down and put his arms around him. He said,

"Don't worry. He is alive now."

11 Then Paul went upstairs again, broke bread, and ate. He spoke to them a long time, until it was early morning. Then he left. 12 They took the young man home alive and were greatly comforted.

The Trip from Troas to Miletus

13 We sailed for the city of Assos. We went first, ahead of Paul. He wanted to join us on the ship there. Paul planned it this way because he wanted to go to Assos by land.

Acts 20:14-21

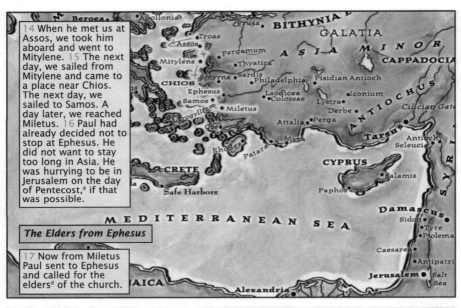

14 When he met us at Assos, we took him aboard and went to Mitylene. 15 The next day, we sailed from Mitylene and came to a place near Chios. The next day, we sailed to Samos. A day later, we reached Miletus. 16 Paul had already decided not to stop at Ephesus. He did not want to stay too long in Asia. He was hurrying to be in Jerusalem on the day of Pentecost,[d] if that was possible.

The Elders from Ephesus

17 Now from Miletus Paul sent to Ephesus and called for the elders[d] of the church.

18 When they came to him, he said,

"You know about my life from the first day I came to Asia. You know the way I lived all the time I was with you. 19 The Jews plotted against me. This troubled me very much. But you know that I always served the Lord. I never thought of myself first, and I often cried.

20 You know I preached to you, and I did not hold back anything that would help you. You know that I taught you in public and in your homes. 21 I warned both Jews and Greeks to change their lives and turn to God. And I told them all to believe in our Lord Jesus.

22 "But now I must obey the Holy Spirit[d] and go to Jerusalem. I don't know what will happen to me there. 23 I know only that in every city the Holy Spirit tells me that troubles and even jail wait for me.

24 I don't care about my own life. The most important thing is that I complete my mission. I want to finish the work that the Lord Jesus gave me—to tell people the Good News[d] about God's grace.

25 "And now, I know that none of you will ever see me again. All the time I was with you, I was preaching the kingdom of God. 26 So today I can tell you one thing that I am sure of: If any of you should be lost, I am not responsible. 27 This is because I have told you everything God wants you to know.

28 Be careful for yourselves and for all the people God has given you. The Holy Spirit gave you the work of caring for this flock. You must be like shepherds to the church of God.[n] This is the church that God bought with his own death.

29 I know that after I leave, some men will come like wild wolves and try to destroy the flock.

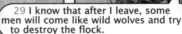

30 Also, men from your own group will rise up and twist the truth. They will lead away followers after them.

31 So be careful! Always remember this: For three years I never stopped warning each of you. I taught you night and day. I often cried over you.

20:28 of God Some Greek copies read "of the Lord."

32 "Now I am putting you in the care of God and the message about his grace. That message is able to give you strength, and it will give you the blessings that God has for all his holy people.

33 When I was with you, I never wanted anyone's money or fine clothes. 34 You know that I always worked to take care of my own needs and the needs of those who were with me. 35 I showed you in all things that you should work as I did and help the weak. I taught you to remember the words of Jesus. He said, 'It is more blessed to give than to receive.' "

36 When Paul had said this, he knelt down with all of them and prayed.

37-38 And they all cried because Paul had said that they would never see him again. They put their arms around him and kissed him. Then they went with him to the ship.

Paul Goes to Jerusalem

1 We all said good-bye to them and left. We sailed straight to Cos island. The next day, we reached Rhodes, and from Rhodes we went to Patara. 2 There we found a ship that was going to Phoenicia. We went aboard and sailed away. 3 We sailed near the island of Cyprus. We could see it to the north, but we sailed on to Syria. We stopped at Tyre because the ship needed to unload its cargo there.

4 We found some followers in Tyre, and we stayed with them for seven days. Through the Holy Spirit[d] they warned Paul not to go to Jerusalem. 5 When we finished our visit, we left and continued our trip. All the followers, even the women and children, came outside the city with us. We all knelt down on the beach and prayed.

6 Then we said good-bye and got on the ship. The followers went back home.

Acts 21:7-14

8 We left Ptolemais and went to the city of Caesarea. There we went into the home of Philip and stayed with him. Philip had the work of telling the Good News.[d] He was one of the seven helpers.[n] 9 He had four unmarried daughters who had the gift of prophesying.[d]

7 We continued our trip from Tyre and arrived at Ptolemais. We greeted the believers there and stayed with them for a day.

10 After we had been there for some time, a prophet named Agabus arrived from Judea. 11 He came to us and borrowed Paul's belt. Then he used the belt to tie his own hands and feet. He said,

"The Holy Spirit says, 'This is how the Jews in Jerusalem will tie up the man who wears this belt. Then they will give him to the non-Jewish people.' "

12 We all heard these words. So we and the people there begged Paul not to go to Jerusalem.

13 But he said,

"Why are you crying and making me so sad? I am ready to be tied up in Jerusalem. And I am ready to die for the Lord Jesus!"

14 We could not persuade him to stay away from Jerusalem. So we stopped begging him and said,

"We pray that what the Lord wants will be done."

21:8 helpers The seven men chosen for a special work described in Acts 6:1-6.

15 After this, we got ready and started on our way to Jerusalem.
16 Some of the followers from Caesarea went with us. They took us to the home of Mnason, a man from Cyprus. Mnason was one of the first followers. They took us to his home so that we could stay with him.

Paul Visits James

17 In Jerusalem the believers were glad to see us.
18 The next day, Paul went with us to visit James. All the elders[d] were there, too.

19 Paul greeted them and told them everything that God had done among the non-Jewish people through him.

Acts 21:20-26

20 When they heard this, they praised God. Then they said to Paul,

"Brother, you can see that many thousands of Jews have become believers. But they think it is very important to obey the law of Moses.

21 These Jews have heard about your teaching. They heard that you tell the Jews who live among non-Jews to leave the law of Moses. They heard that you tell them not to circumcise[d] their children and not to obey Jewish customs. 22 What should we do? The Jewish believers here will learn that you have come.

23 So we will tell you what to do: Four of our men have made a promise to God. 24 Take these men with you and share in their cleansing ceremony.[n] Pay their expenses. Then they can shave their heads.[n]

Do this and it will prove to everyone that what they have heard about you is not true. They will see that you follow the law of Moses in your own life. 25 We have already sent a letter to the non-Jewish believers. The letter said: 'Do not eat food that has been offered to idols. Do not taste blood. Do not eat animals that have been strangled. Do not take part in any kind of sexual sin.' "

26 Then Paul took the four men with him. The next day, he shared in the cleansing ceremony. Then he went to the Temple.[d] Paul announced the time when the days of the cleansing ceremony would be finished. On the last day an offering would be given for each of the men.

21:24 cleansing ceremony The special things Jews did to end the Nazirite promise.
21:24 shave their heads The Jews did this to show that their promise was finished.

27 The seven days were almost over. But some Jews from Asia saw Paul at the Temple. They caused all the people to be upset, and they grabbed Paul. 28 They shouted,

"Men of Israel, help us! This is the man who goes everywhere teaching things that are against the law of Moses, against our people, and against this Temple. And now he has brought some Greek men into the Temple. He has made this holy place unclean!"d

29 (The Jews said this because they had seen Trophimus with Paul in Jerusalem. Trophimus was a man from Ephesus. The Jews thought that Paul had brought him into the Temple.)

30 All the people in Jerusalem became very upset. They ran and took Paul and dragged him out of the Temple. The Temple doors were closed immediately.

31 The people were about to kill Paul. Now the commander of the Roman army in Jerusalem learned that there was trouble in the whole city.

32 Immediately he ran to the place where the crowd was gathered. He brought officers and soldiers with him, and the people saw them. So they stopped beating Paul.

Acts 21:33-40

33 The commander went to Paul and arrested him. He told his soldiers to tie Paul with two chains. Then he asked, "Who is this man? What has he done wrong?" 34 Some in the crowd were yelling one thing, and some were yelling another. Because of all this confusion and shouting, the commander could not learn what had happened.

So he ordered the soldiers to take Paul to the army building. 35-36 The whole mob was following them. When the soldiers came to the steps, they had to carry Paul. They did this because the people were ready to hurt him. They were shouting,

"Kill him!"

37 The soldiers were about to take Paul into the army building. But he spoke to the commander,

"May I say something to you?"

The commander said,

"Do you speak Greek? 38 I thought you were the Egyptian who started some trouble against the government not long ago. He led 4,000 killers out to the desert."

39 Paul said,

"No, I am a Jew from Tarsus in the country of Cilicia. I am a citizen of that important city. Please, let me speak to the people."

40 The commander gave permission, so Paul stood on the steps. He waved with his hand so that the people would be quiet. When there was silence, Paul spoke to them in the Jewish language."

21:40 **Jewish language** Aramaic, the language of the Jews in the first century.

1 Paul said, "Brothers and fathers, listen to me! I will make my defense to you."

Chapter

22

Paul Speaks to the People

2 When the Jews heard him speaking the Jewish language,[n] they became very quiet. Paul said,

3 "I am a Jew. I was born in Tarsus in the country of Cilicia.

I grew up in this city. I was a student of Gamaliel.[n] He carefully taught me everything about the law of our ancestors. I was very serious about serving God, just as are all of you here today. 4 I hurt the people who followed the Way of Jesus. Some of them were even killed. I arrested men and women and put them in jail.

5 The high priest and the whole council of Jewish elders can tell you that this is true. These leaders gave me letters to the Jewish brothers in Damascus. So I was going there to arrest these people and bring them back to Jerusalem to be punished.

6 "But something happened to me on my way to Damascus. It was about noon when I came near Damascus. Suddenly a bright light from heaven flashed all around me. 7 I fell to the ground and heard a voice saying, 'Saul, Saul, why are you doing things against me?'

8 I asked, 'Who are you, Lord?' The voice said, 'I am Jesus from Nazareth. I am the One you are trying to hurt.' 9 The men who were with me did not understand the voice. But they saw the light. 10 I said, 'What shall I do, Lord?' The Lord answered, 'Get up and go to Damascus. There you will be told about all the things I have planned for you to do.' 11 I could not see, because the bright light had made me blind. So the men led me into Damascus.

22:2 Jewish language Aramaic, the language of the Jews in the first century.
22:3 Gamaliel A very important teacher of the Pharisees, a Jewish religious group (Acts 5:34).

12 "There a man named Ananias came to me. He was a religious man; he obeyed the law of Moses. All the Jews who lived there respected him. 13 Ananias came to me, stood by me, and said, 'Brother Saul, see again!' Immediately I was able to see him.

14 Ananias told me, 'The God of our fathers chose you long ago. He chose you to know his plan. He chose you to see the Righteous One and to hear words from him. 15 You will be his witness to all people. You will tell them about the things you have seen and heard. 16 Now, why wait any longer? Get up, be baptized, and wash your sins away. Do this, trusting in him to save you.'

17 "Later, I returned to Jerusalem. I was praying in the Temple,[d] and I saw a vision. 18 I saw the Lord saying to me, 'Hurry! Leave Jerusalem now! The people here will not accept the truth about me.'

19 But I said, 'Lord, they know that in every synagogue[d] I put the believers in jail and beat them. 20 They also know that I was there when Stephen, your witness, was killed. I stood there and agreed that they should kill him. I even held the coats of the men who were killing him!'

21 But the Lord said to me, 'Leave now. I will send you far away to the non-Jewish people.' "

22 The crowd listened to Paul until he said this. Then they began shouting,

"Get rid of him! A man like this doesn't deserve to live!"

23 They shouted and threw off their coats." They threw dust into the air."
24 Then the commander ordered the soldiers to take Paul into the army building and beat him. The commander wanted to make Paul tell why the people were shouting against him like this.

25 So the soldiers were tying him up, preparing to beat him. But Paul said to an officer there,

"Do you have the right to beat a Roman citizen" who has not been proven guilty?"

22:23 **threw off their coats** This showed that the Jews were very angry at Paul.
22:23 **threw dust into the air** This showed even greater anger.
22:25 **Roman citizen** Roman law said that Roman citizens must not be beaten before they had a trial.

Acts 22:26-30

Chapter 23

1 Paul looked at the Jewish council and said,

"Brothers, I have lived my life in a good way before God up to this day."

2 Ananias,[n] the high priest, heard this and told the men who were standing near Paul to hit him on his mouth.

3 Paul said to Ananias,

"God will hit you too! You are like a wall that has been painted white! You sit there and judge me, using the law of Moses. But you are telling them to hit me, and that is against the law."

4 The men standing near Paul said to him,

"You cannot talk like that to God's high priest! You are insulting him!"

5 Paul said,

"Brothers, I did not know this man was the high priest. It is written in the Scriptures,[d] 'You must not curse a leader of your people.' "[n]

23:2 Ananias This is not the same man named Ananias in Acts 22:12.
23:5 'You . . . people.' Quotation from Exodus 22:28.

Acts 23:6-11

6 Some of the men in the meeting were Sadducees,[d] and others were Pharisees.[d] So Paul shouted to them,

"My brothers, I am a Pharisee and my father was a Pharisee! I am on trial here because I hope that people will rise from death!"

7 When Paul said this, there was an argument between the Pharisees and the Sadducees. The group was divided. 8 (The Sadducees believe that after people die, they cannot live again. The Sadducees also teach that there are no angels or spirits. But the Pharisees believe in them all.) 9 So there was a great uproar. Some of the teachers of the law, who were Pharisees, stood up and argued,

"We find nothing wrong with this man! Maybe an angel or a spirit did speak to him."

10 The argument was beginning to turn into a fight. The commander was afraid that the Jews would tear Paul to pieces. So the commander told the soldiers to go down and take Paul away and put him in the army building.

11 The next night the Lord came and stood by Paul. He said,

"Be brave! You have told people in Jerusalem about me. You must do the same in Rome also."

12 In the morning some of the Jews made a plan to kill Paul. They made a promise that they would not eat or drink anything until they had killed him. 13 There were more than 40 Jews who made this plan. 14 They went and talked to the leading priests and the Jewish elders. They said,
"We have made a promise to ourselves that we will not eat or drink until we have killed Paul! 15 So this is what we want you to do: Send a message to the commander to bring Paul out to you. Tell him you want to ask Paul more questions. We will be waiting to kill him while he is on the way here."

16 But Paul's nephew heard about this plan. He went to the army building and told Paul about it.
17 Then Paul called one of the officers and said,
"Take this young man to the commander. He has a message for him."

18 So the officer brought Paul's nephew to the commander. The officer said,

"The prisoner, Paul, asked me to bring this young man to you. He wants to tell you something."

19 The commander led the young man to a place where they could be alone. The commander asked,

"What do you want to tell me?"

20 The young man said,

"The Jews have decided to ask you to bring Paul down to their council meeting tomorrow. They want you to think that they are going to ask him more questions.

21 But don't believe them! There are more than 40 men who are hiding and waiting to kill Paul. They have all made a promise not to eat or drink until they have killed him!

Now they are waiting for you to agree."

"Don't tell anyone that you have told me about their plan."

22 The commander sent the young man away. He said to him,

Paul Is Sent to Caesarea

23 Then the commander called two officers. He said to them,

"I need some men to go to Caesarea. Get 200 soldiers ready. Also, get 70 horsemen and 200 men with spears. Be ready to leave at nine o'clock tonight.

24 Get some horses for Paul to ride. He must be taken to Governor Felix safely."

25 And he wrote a letter that said:

From Claudius Lysias. To the Most Excellent Governor Felix:

Greetings. 27 The Jews had taken this man, and they planned to kill him. But I learned that he is a Roman citizen, so I went with my soldiers and saved him. 28 I wanted to know why they were accusing him. So I brought him before their council meeting. 29 I learned that the Jews said Paul did some things that were wrong. But these charges were about their own laws. And no charge was worthy of jail or death. 30 I was told that some of the Jews were planning to kill Paul. So I sent him to you at once. I also told those Jews to tell you what they have against him.

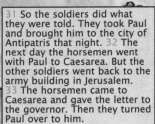

31 So the soldiers did what they were told. They took Paul and brought him to the city of Antipatris that night. 32 The next day the horsemen went with Paul to Caesarea. But the other soldiers went back to the army building in Jerusalem. 33 The horsemen came to Caesarea and gave the letter to the governor. Then they turned Paul over to him.

34 The governor read the letter. Then he asked Paul, "What area are you from?" He learned that Paul was from Cilicia. 35 He said,

"I will hear your case when those who are against you come here too."

Then the governor gave orders for Paul to be kept under guard in the palace. (This building had been built by Herod.)

Chapter

24

The Jews Accuse Paul

1 Five days later Ananias, the high priest, went to the city of Caesarea. With him were some of the Jewish elders and a lawyer named Tertullus. They had come to make charges against Paul before the governor. 2 Paul was called into the meeting, and Tertullus began to accuse him, saying:

"Most Excellent Felix! Our people enjoy much peace because of you, and many wrong things in our country are being made right through your wise help. 3 We accept these things always and in every place. And we are thankful for them. 4 But I do not want to take any more of your time. I beg you to be kind and listen to our few words.

5 "This man is a troublemaker. He makes trouble among the Jews everywhere in the world. He is a leader of the Nazarene[d] group. 6 Also, he was trying to make the Temple[d] unclean,[d] but we stopped him. [And we wanted to judge him by our own law.

7 But the officer Lysias came and used much force to take him from us. And Lysias commanded his people to come to you to accuse us.][n] 8 You can decide if all these things are true. Ask him some questions yourself."

9 The other Jews agreed and said that all of this was true. 10 The governor made a sign for Paul to speak. So Paul said,

"Governor Felix, I know that you have been a judge over this nation for a long time. So I am happy to defend myself before you.

11 I went to worship in Jerusalem only 12 days ago. You can learn for yourself that this is true. 12 Those who are accusing me did not find me arguing with anyone in the Temple. I was not stirring up the people. And I was not making trouble in the Temple or in the synagogues[d] or in the city.

13 They cannot prove the things they are saying against me now.

24:6-7 And . . . us. Some Greek copies do not contain the bracketed text.

14 "But I will tell you this: I worship the God of our ancestors as a follower of the Way of Jesus. The Jews say that the Way of Jesus is not the right way. But I believe everything that is taught in the law of Moses and that is written in the books of the Prophets.ᵈ 15 I have the same hope in God that they have—the hope that all people, good and bad, will be raised from death.

16 This is why I always try to do what I believe is right before God and men. 17 "I was away from Jerusalem for several years. I went back there to bring money to my people and to offer sacrifices.

18 I was doing this when they found me in the Temple. I had finished the cleansing ceremony. I had not made any trouble; no people were gathering around me.

19 But some Jews from Asia were there. They should be here, standing before you. If I have really done anything wrong, they are the ones who should accuse me. 20 Or ask these Jews here if they found any wrong in me when I stood before the Jewish council in Jerusalem.

21 But I did say one thing when I stood before them: 'You are judging me today because I believe that people will rise from death!'"

22 Felix already understood much about the Way of Jesus. He stopped the trial and said,

"When commander Lysias comes here, I will decide about your case."

23 Felix told the officer to keep Paul guarded. But he told the officer to give Paul some freedom and to let his friends bring what he needed.

Paul Speaks to Felix and His Wife

24 After some days Felix came with his wife, Drusilla, who was a Jew. He asked for Paul to be brought to him. He listened to Paul talk about believing in Christ Jesus. 25 But Felix became afraid when Paul spoke about things like right living, self-control, and the time when God will judge the world. He said,

"Go away now. When I have more time, I will call for you."

26 At the same time Felix hoped that Paul would give him some money. So he sent for Paul often and talked with him. 27 But after two years, Porcius Festus became governor. Felix was no longer governor, but he had left Paul in prison to please the Jews.

Chapter 25

Paul Asks to See Caesar

1 Three days after Festus became governor, he went from Caesarea to Jerusalem. 2 There the leading priests and the important Jewish leaders made charges against Paul before Festus.

3 They asked Festus to do something for them; they wanted him to send Paul back to Jerusalem. (They had a plan to kill Paul on the way.) 4 But Festus answered,

"No!

Paul will be kept in Caesarea. I will return there soon myself. 5 Some of your leaders should go with me. They can accuse the man there in Caesarea, if he has really done something wrong."

6 Festus stayed in Jerusalem another eight or ten days. Then he went back to Caesarea. The next day he told the soldiers to bring Paul before him. Festus was seated on the judge's seat

7 when Paul came into the room. The Jews who had come from Jerusalem stood around him. They started making serious charges against Paul. But they could not prove any of them. 8 This is what Paul said to defend himself:

"I have done nothing wrong against the Jewish law, against the Temple,ᵈ or against Caesar!"ᵈ

9 But Festus wanted to please the Jews. So he asked Paul,

"Do you want to go to Jerusalem? Do you want me to judge you there on these charges?"

10 Paul said,

"I am standing at Caesar's judgment seat now. This is where I should be judged! I have done nothing wrong to the Jews; you know this is true. 11 If I have done something wrong and the law says I must die, I do not ask to be saved from death. But if these charges are not true, then no one can give me to them.

No! I want Caesar to hear my case!"

12 Festus talked about this with the people who advised him. Then he said,

"You have asked to see Caesar; so you will go to Caesar!"

Paul Before King Agrippa

13 A few days later King Agrippa and Bernice came to Caesarea to visit Festus. 14 They stayed there for some time, and Festus told the king about Paul's case. Festus said,

"There is a man that Felix left in prison. 15 When I went to Jerusalem, the leading priests and the Jewish elders there made charges against him. They wanted me to sentence him to death.

16 But I answered, 'When a man is accused of a crime, Romans do not hand him over just to please someone. The man must be allowed to face his accusers and defend himself against their charges.'

17 So these Jews came here to Caesarea for the trial. And I did not waste time. The next day I sat on the judge's seat and commanded that the man be brought in. 18 The Jews stood up and accused him. But they did not accuse him of any serious crime as I thought they would.

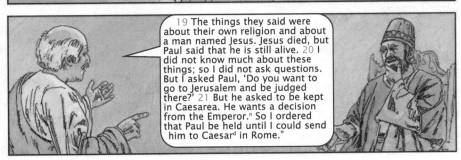

19 The things they said were about their own religion and about a man named Jesus. Jesus died, but Paul said that he is still alive. 20 I did not know much about these things; so I did not ask questions. But I asked Paul, 'Do you want to go to Jerusalem and be judged there?' 21 But he asked to be kept in Caesarea. He wants a decision from the Emperor.ⁿ So I ordered that Paul be held until I could send him to Caesarᵈ in Rome."

25:21 Emperor The ruler of the Roman Empire, which was almost all the world.

22 Agrippa said to Festus,

"I would like to hear this man, too."

Festus said,

"Tomorrow, you will hear him!"

23 The next day Agrippa and Bernice appeared. They dressed and acted like very important people. Agrippa and Bernice, the army leaders, and the important men of Caesarea went into the judgment room. Then Festus ordered the soldiers to bring Paul in. 24 Festus said,

"King Agrippa and all who are gathered here with us, you see this man. All the Jewish people, here and in Jerusalem, have complained to me about him. They shout that he should not live any longer.

25 When I judged him, I could find nothing wrong. I found no reason to order his death. But he asked to be judged by Caesar. So I decided to send him. 26 But I have nothing definite to write the Emperor about him. So I have brought him before all of you—especially you, King Agrippa. I hope that you can question him and give me something to write. 27 I think it is foolish to send a prisoner to Caesar without telling what the charges are against him."

1 Agrippa said to Paul,

"You may now speak to defend yourself."

chapter

26

Paul Defends Himself

Then Paul raised his hand and began to speak. 2 He said,

"King Agrippa, I will answer all the charges that the Jews make against me. I think it is a blessing that I can stand here before you today. 3 I am very happy to talk to you, because you know so much about all the Jewish customs and the things that the Jews argue about. Please listen to me patiently.

4 "All the Jews know about my whole life. They know the way I lived from the beginning in my own country and later in Jerusalem.

5 They have known me for a long time. If they want to, they can tell you that I was a good Pharisee.d And the Pharisees obey the laws of the Jewish religion more carefully than any other group of Jewish people. 6 Now I am on trial because I hope for the promise that God made to our ancestors.

7 This is the promise that the 12 tribesd of our people hope to receive. For this hope the Jews serve God day and night. My king, the Jews have accused me because I hope for this same promise! 8 Why do any of you people think it is impossible for God to raise people from death?

125

9 "I too thought I ought to do many things against Jesus from Nazareth. 10 And in Jerusalem I did many things against God's people. The leading priests gave me the power to put many of them in jail. When they were being killed, I agreed that it was a good thing. 11 In every synagogue,[d] I often punished them. I tried to make them say evil things against Jesus.

I was so angry against them that I even went to other cities to find them and punish them. 12 "One time the leading priests gave me permission and the power to go to Damascus. 13 On the way there, at noon, I saw a light from heaven.

The light was brighter than the sun. It flashed all around me and the men who were traveling with me. 14 We all fell to the ground. Then I heard a voice speaking to me in the Jewish language.[n] The voice said, 'Saul, Saul, why are you doing things against me? You are only hurting yourself by fighting me.' 15 I said, 'Who are you, Lord?' The Lord said, 'I am Jesus. I am the One you are trying to hurt.

16 Stand up! I have chosen you to be my servant. You will be my witness—you will tell people the things that you have seen and the things that I will show you. This is why I have come to you today. 17 I will not let your own people hurt you. And I will keep you safe from the non-Jewish people too. These are the people I am sending you to.

18 I send you to open their eyes that they may turn away from darkness to the light. I send you that they may turn away from the power of Satan and turn to God. Then their sins can be forgiven and they can have a place with those people who have been made holy by believing in me.'

26:14 Jewish language Aramaic, the language of the Jews in the first century.

19 "King Agrippa, after I had this vision from heaven, I obeyed it. 20 I began telling people that they should change their hearts and lives and turn to God. I told them to do things to show that they really had changed. I told this first to those in Damascus, then in Jerusalem and in every part of Judea, and also to the non-Jewish people. 21 This is why the Jews took me and were trying to kill me in the Temple.[d]

22 But God helped me and is still helping me today. With God's help I am standing here today and telling all people what I have seen. But I am saying nothing new. I am saying what Moses and the prophets[d] said would happen. 23 They said that the Christ[d] would die and be the first to rise from death. They said that the Christ would bring light to the Jewish and non-Jewish people."

Paul Tries to Persuade Agrippa

24 While Paul was saying these things to defend himself, Festus said loudly,

"Paul, you are out of your mind! Too much study has driven you crazy!"

25 Paul said,

"Most Excellent Festus, I am not crazy. My words are true. They are not the words of a foolish man.

26 King Agrippa knows about these things. I can speak freely to him. I know that he has heard about all of these things. They did not happen off in a corner. 27 King Agrippa, do you believe what the prophets[d] wrote? I know you believe!"

28 King Agrippa said to Paul,

"Do you think you can persuade me to become a Christian in such a short time?"

29 Paul said,

"Whether it is a short or a long time, I pray to God that not only you but every person listening to me today would be saved and be like me—except for these chains I have!"

30 Then King Agrippa, Governor Festus, Bernice, and all the people sitting with them stood up 31 and left the room. They were talking to each other. They said,

"There is no reason why this man should die or be put in jail."

32 And Agrippa said to Festus,

"We could let this man go free, but he has asked Caesar[d] to hear his case."

Chapter 27

Paul Sails for Rome

1 It was decided that we would sail for Italy. An officer named Julius, who served in the Emperor's[n] army, guarded Paul and some other prisoners.

2 We got on a ship and left. The ship was from the city of Adramyttium and was about to sail to different ports in Asia. Aristarchus, a man from the city of Thessalonica in Macedonia, went with us.

3 The next day we came to Sidon. Julius was very good to Paul. He gave Paul freedom to go visit his friends, who took care of his needs. 4 We left Sidon and sailed close to the island of Cyprus because the wind was blowing against us.

27:1 Emperor The ruler of the Roman Empire, which was almost all the world.

5 We went across the sea by Cilicia and Pamphylia. Then we came to the city of Myra, in Lycia. 6 There the officer found a ship from Alexandria that was going to Italy. So he put us on it.
7 We sailed slowly for many days. We had a hard time reaching Cnidus because the wind was blowing against us. We could not go any farther that way. So we sailed by the south side of the island of Crete near Salmone.

8 We sailed along the coast, but the sailing was hard. Then we came to a place called Safe Harbors, near the city of Lasea.
9 But we had lost much time. It was now dangerous to sail, because it was already after the Day of Cleansing.[n]

So Paul warned them,

10 "Men, I can see there will be a lot of trouble on this trip. The ship and the things in the ship will be lost. Even our lives may be lost!"

11 But the captain and the owner of the ship did not agree with Paul. So the officer did not believe Paul. Instead, the officer believed what the captain and owner of the ship said.

27:9 Day of Cleansing An important Jewish holy day in the fall of the year. This was the time of year that bad storms happened on the sea.

12 And that harbor was not a good place for the ship to stay for the winter. So most of the men decided that the ship should leave. The men hoped we could go to Phoenix. The ship could stay there for the winter. (Phoenix was a city on the island of Crete. It had a harbor which faced southwest and northwest.)

The Storm

13 Then a good wind began to blow from the south. The men on the ship thought, "This is the wind we wanted, and now we have it!" So they pulled up the anchor. We sailed very close to the island of Crete. 14 But then a very strong wind named the "Northeaster" came from the island.

15 This wind took the ship and carried it away. The ship could not sail against it. So we stopped trying and let the wind blow us. 16 We went below a small island named Cauda. Then we were able to bring in the lifeboat, but it was very hard to do.

17 After the men took the lifeboat in, they tied ropes around the ship to hold it together. The men were afraid that the ship would hit the sandbanks of Syrtis.[n] So they lowered the sail and let the wind carry the ship.

27:17 Syrtis Shallow area in the sea near the Libyan coast.

18 The next day the storm was blowing us so hard that the men threw out some of the cargo. 19 A day later they threw out the ship's equipment.

20 For many days we could not see the sun or the stars. The storm was very bad. We lost all hope of staying alive—we thought we would die.

21 The men had gone without food for a long time. Then one day Paul stood up before them and said,

"Men, I told you not to leave Crete. You should have listened to me. Then you would not have all this trouble and loss. 22 But now I tell you to cheer up. None of you will die! But the ship will be lost.

23 "Last night an angel from God came to me. This is the God I worship. I am his. 24 God's angel said, 'Paul, do not be afraid! You must stand before Caesar.[d] And God has given you this promise: He will save the lives of all those men sailing with you.'

25 So men, be cheerful! I trust in God. Everything will happen as his angel told me. 26 But we will crash on an island."

27 On the fourteenth night we were floating around in the Adriatic Sea.[n] The sailors thought we were close to land.

28 They threw a rope into the water with a weight on the end of it. They found that the water was 120 feet deep.

They went a little farther and threw the rope in again. It was 90 feet deep.

29 The sailors were afraid that we would hit the rocks, so they threw four anchors into the water. Then they prayed for daylight to come.

27:27 Adriatic Sea The sea between Greece and Italy, including the central Mediterranean.

30 Some of the sailors wanted to leave the ship, and they lowered the lifeboat. These sailors wanted the other men to think that they were throwing more anchors from the front of the ship. 31 But Paul told the officer and the other soldiers,

"If these men do not stay in the ship, your lives cannot be saved!"

32 So the soldiers cut the ropes and let the lifeboat fall into the water.

33 Just before dawn Paul began persuading all the people to eat something. He said,

"For the past 14 days you have been waiting and watching. You have not eaten. 34 Now I beg you to eat something. You need it to stay alive. None of you will lose even one hair off your heads."

35 After he said this, Paul took some bread and thanked God for it before all of them. He broke off a piece and began eating.

36 All the men felt better. They all started eating too. 37 (There were 276 people on the ship.)

Acts 27:38-44

38 We ate all we wanted. Then we began making the ship lighter by throwing the grain into the sea.

The Ship Is Destroyed

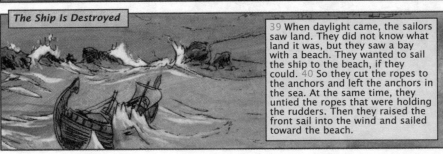

39 When daylight came, the sailors saw land. They did not know what land it was, but they saw a bay with a beach. They wanted to sail the ship to the beach, if they could. 40 So they cut the ropes to the anchors and left the anchors in the sea. At the same time, they untied the ropes that were holding the rudders. Then they raised the front sail into the wind and sailed toward the beach.

41 But the ship hit a sandbank. The front of the ship stuck there and could not move. Then the big waves began to break the back of the ship to pieces. 42 The soldiers decided to kill the prisoners so that none of them could swim away and escape. 43 But Julius, the officer, wanted to let Paul live. He did not allow the soldiers to kill the prisoners. Instead he ordered everyone who could swim to jump into the water and swim to land. 44 The rest used wooden boards or pieces of the ship. And this is how all the people made it safely to land.

Chapter 28

Paul on the Island of Malta

1 When we were safe on land, we learned that the island was called Malta. 2 It was raining and very cold. But the people who lived there were very good to us. They made us a fire and welcomed all of us.

3 Paul gathered a pile of sticks for the fire. He was putting them on the fire when a poisonous snake came out because of the heat and bit him on the hand.

4 The people living on the island saw the snake hanging from Paul's hand. They said to each other,

"This man must be a murderer! He did not die in the sea, but Justice" does not want him to live."

5 But Paul shook the snake off into the fire. He was not hurt.

28:4 Justice The people thought there was a god named Justice who would punish bad people.

6 The people thought that Paul would swell up or fall down dead. The people waited and watched him for a long time, but nothing bad happened to him. So they changed their minds about Paul. Now they said,

"He is a god!"

7 There were some fields around there owned by a very important man on the island. His name was Publius. He welcomed us into his home and was very good to us. We stayed in his house for three days.

8 Publius' father was very sick with a fever and dysentery.[n] But Paul went to him and prayed.

Then he put his hands on the man and healed him.

9 After this, all the other sick people on the island came to Paul, and he healed them, too.

10-11 The people on the island gave us many honors. We stayed there three months. When we were ready to leave, they gave us the things we needed.

28:8 dysentery A sickness like diarrhea.

Paul Goes to Rome

We got on a ship from Alexandria. The ship had stayed on the island during the winter. On the front of the ship was the sign of the twin gods.[n] 12 We stopped at Syracuse for three days and then left. 13 From there we sailed to Rhegium. The next day a wind began to blow from the southwest, so we were able to leave. A day later we came to Puteoli.

14 We found some believers there, and they asked us to stay with them for a week. Finally, we came to Rome. 15 The believers in Rome heard that we were there. They came out as far as the Market of Appius[n] and the Three Inns[n] to meet us.

When Paul saw them, he was encouraged and thanked God.

Paul in Rome

16 Then we arrived at Rome. There, Paul was allowed to live alone. But a soldier stayed with him to guard him.

28:10-11 **twin gods** Statues of Castor and Pollux, gods in old Greek tales.
28:15 **Market of Appius** A town about 27 miles from Rome.
28:15 **Three Inns** A town about 30 miles from Rome.

137

Acts 28:17-22

17 Three days later Paul sent for the Jewish leaders there. When they came together, he said,

"Brothers, I have done nothing against our people. I have done nothing against the customs of our fathers. But I was arrested in Jerusalem and given to the Romans. 18 The Romans asked me many questions. But they could find no reason why I should be killed. They wanted to let me go free,

19 but the Jews there did not want that. So I had to ask to come to Rome to have my trial before Caesar.d But I have no charge to bring against my own people.

20 That is why I wanted to see you and talk with you. I am bound with this chain because I believe in the hope of Israel."

21 The Jews answered Paul,

"We have received no letters from Judea about you. None of our Jewish brothers who have come from there brought news about you or told us anything bad about you.

22 We want to hear your ideas. We know that people everywhere are speaking against this religious group."

23 Paul and the Jews chose a day for a meeting. On that day many more of the Jews met with Paul at the place he was staying. Paul spoke to them all day long, explaining the kingdom of God to them. He tried to persuade them to believe these things about Jesus. He used the law of Moses and the writings of the prophets[d] to do this. 24 Some of the Jews believed what Paul said, but others did not. 25 So they argued, and the Jews were ready to leave. But Paul said one more thing to them:

"The Holy Spirit[d] spoke the truth to your fathers through Isaiah the prophet. He said,

26 'Go to this people and say: You will listen and listen, but you will not understand. You will look and look, but you will not learn.

27 For these people have become stubborn. They don't hear with their ears. And they have closed their eyes. Otherwise, they might really understand what they see with their eyes and hear with their ears. They might really understand in their minds. If they did this, they would come back to me and be forgiven.' Isaiah 6:9-10

28 "I want you Jews to know that God has also sent his salvation to the non-Jewish people. They will listen!"

29 [After Paul said this, the Jews left. They were arguing very much with each other.][n]

30 Paul stayed two full years in his own rented house. He welcomed all people who came and visited him. 31 He preached about the kingdom of God and taught about the Lord Jesus Christ. He was very bold, and no one stopped him.

28:29 After . . . other. Some Greek copies do not contain the bracketed text.

People I Want
to Pray For

Situations
I Want to Pray For

Answered
Prayers

_____   _____
_____   _____
_____   _____
_____   _____
_____   _____
_____   _____
_____   _____
_____   _____
_____   _____
_____   _____
_____   _____
_____   _____
_____   _____
_____   _____
_____   _____
_____   _____
_____   _____
_____   _____
_____   _____
_____   _____
_____   _____

Notes

Notes

Notes

Notes

Notes

Notes